Niagara-on-the-Lake Guidebook

• • •

John L. Field

Self-guided tours of the OLD TOWN
and the neighbouring area
on foot, by bicycle or car,
routes and distances shown,
to help our visitors
enjoy and remember
our town

•

4th (revised) printing – 1989

ISBN 0 - 9691751 - 0 - 8

Cover Picture: Clock Tower and 1847 Court House

Printed by the Renown Printing Co. Ltd.
4795 Kent Avenue
Niagara Falls, Ontario L2H 1J5

To PICKLE
faithful companion
on all these outings

Arriving in style at the Queen's Royal Hotel. (see page 24)

A WORD TO THE READER

The idea of producing a guidebook to our town was suggested to me in February 1983 by the proprietor of the Old Niagara Bookshop. Many of her customers had asked for a book that would describe what was worth seeing in Niagara-on-the-Lake, and where to find it. This project seemed to be suited to my talents, for I had already conducted some seventy tours of the town, usually on behalf of the Niagara Historical Society. Accordingly, I planned eight tours, made the other necessary preparations for breaking into print, and hopefully launched my Guidebook on May 18, 1984. Since then it has gone through several re-printings, and with each I have been able to update certain information and to add a few new pictures.

Of the eight tours, seven may be covered on foot. The eighth one goes round the edge of the old town, and, being somewhat longer, ought to be undertaken by bicycle or automobile. The tours do not have to be done in the order they may appear, but they are arranged in logical sequence, starting with the centre of town and working out from there. In each case the return route is different from the "out" route, so that on the way back you pass through a different area. You don't really have to walk, bicycle, or drive if you prefer not to; simply read the Guidebook with care, and you will become acquainted with old Niagara.

That brings me to the matter of its name. "Niagara" was an Indian word that was probably applied to this general area. When the United Empire Loyalists moved to this side of the river, the settlement that grew up here had several informal names until Lieutenant-Governor John Graves Simcoe arrived here in 1792. He decided to make this little village the capital of Upper Canada, and renamed it "Newark" after a town in Nottinghamshire. Once Simcoe was out of the way and safely back in England, the townspeople, a stubborn lot, prevailed on the Upper Canada legislature to restore the name "Niagara" in 1798.

By the beginning of this century, the post office was experiencing some confusion between the city of Niagara Falls and our own Niagara. To solve this, they bestowed on us in 1902 the postal address of "Niagara-on-the-Lake". Many people assumed that this was the name of the town and proceeded to use it freely, but we were still "Niagara" in the municipal records. This continued unchanged till 1970, when Ontario adopted regional government. At that time the old town of Niagara was combined with the surrounding Township of Niagara (which included the villages of Queenston, St. Davids, and Virgil) to form the regional town of Niagara-on-the-Lake. Finally this was our proper legal name.

Throughout the Guidebook I have therefore referred to our town as "Niagara" because it has had that name longer than any other. This has also the advantage of brevity, and it is the one we townspeople use in everyday conversation. Local memories are long here in Niagara: for example, when we talk about "the war" we mean the War of 1812. There is reason to remember it: the Americans captured Niagara and occupied it during the entire summer of 1813, putting it to the torch as they retreated.

A great many people have assisted me with my Guidebook, by answering questions or suggesting where I might find the information I needed. In referring to specific houses I have taken the liberty of calling them by the names that Peter Stokes used in his book "Old Niagara on the Lake" (1971) because these have come into common usage. The Niagara Historical Society has permitted me to reproduce a number of old pictures from their files, thus adding reality to the story. My wife Peg always extended her quiet encouragement and thoughtful suggestions while I laboured at my task. Finally, my thanks to Pickle, our lively Dalmatian, who helped me to reconnoitre these tours, and passed away in the summer of 1986.

Box 146, Delatre Lodge   John L. Field
Niagara-on-the-Lake
Ontario   L0S 1J0

Contents

CENTRE TOWN

(10 blocks)

This tour is your introduction to the town. In it we look at two churches, our oldest cemetery, one of our main hotels, the War Memorial, and a building of much character, our Court House. We will start with the last-named; put your car in the parking lot behind it, and walk around to view it from the front.

The Court House was designed by William Thomas, a talented architect who was also responsible for the Don Jail and the St. Lawrence Hall in Toronto. He had the problem of fitting this building between existing structures, consequently he placed the finest detail on its front exposure. The Niagara Court House was completed in 1847, the third to be constructed in town, replacing one built on the south-east edge of town after the War of 1812.

From the beginning of the century Niagara had been the centre for the District of Niagara, which included three counties. With the increase in population the government was about to make the counties rather than the original districts the operative units for area administration. This building was planned in the expectation that the town would shortly assume the role of county seat for Lincoln. To the great disappointment of the townspeople, St. Catharines, a newer fast-growing town on the Welland Canal, won out over Niagara. As a result the building that was intended to be a court house held that honour only briefly, and became instead the Town Hall for Niagara in 1862.

Since then the interior of the building, remodelled as need arose, has quite lost the appearance of a court house. The Lord Mayor*, the town clerk and the municipal staff have had their offices there. For a time there was a covered market at the rear; the library, fire department, police, and historical society each occupied some space. The Works Department used some of the basement, and the high school had a rifle range there.

Early this century the Sovereign Bank had its office on the main floor at the left, and the post office was across the hall. In wartime the Red Cross had its headquarters here, followed by the Senior Citizens' Centre and recent occupants like the town Bicentennial Committee and the Court House Restoration Fund-Raising Office. The large hall upstairs has been used for public meetings, dances and other social events, badminton, school commencements, antique shows, and the humble beginnings of the Shaw Festival in 1962. The kitchen located between the large hall and the small hall at the rear has been useful for many of these functions. Even the front steps have a bonus for the photographer: a new town council or a visiting group of V.I.P.s can be recorded there, with the certainty that everbody's face will appear in the picture.

When regional government came into force in 1970, the Town of Niagara and the Township of Niagara were merged to become the "Regional Town of Niagara-on-the-Lake". Its offices were set up in the existing Township of Niagara offices in Virgil, and the 1847 building again lost its main function. By then the structure was beginning to show its age; some regarded it as a "white elephant", now neither Court House nor Town Hall.

Fortunately there was strong local feeling in favour of saving the old building. In this the town council took the lead: negotiations were conducted to secure grants from provincial and federal governments, and exploratory talks took place with officials of Parks Canada and the Shaw

---

*Sometime in the past the mayors of Niagara began to refer to themselves as "lord mayor" on the grounds that our town was the first capital of Upper Canada. No documentary evidence to support this has been found, but nobody has tried to disprove it.

Festival as to their future use of the building. The general aim of the project was to restore its exterior, and to renovate the interior so as to make it a functional building that would pay its way. The cost of the work, as drawn up by the architectural firm of MacDonald and Zuberec of St. Catharines, was $1,420,000. As soon as the decision to proceed was made, a local committee was formed to raise additional funds by public and private donations, as well as to organize money-raising events of all types.

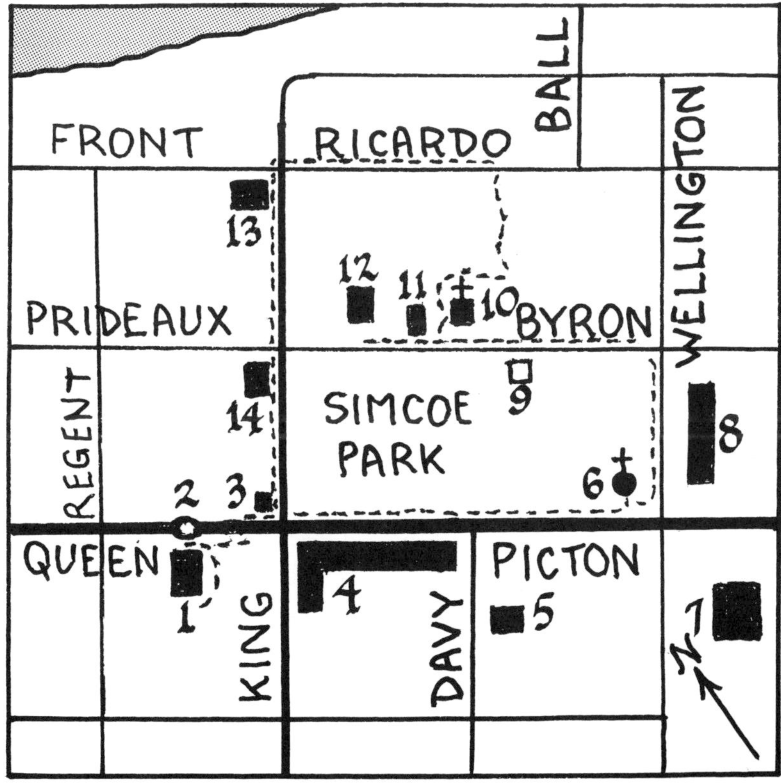

Tour 1

1. Court House
2. Clock Tower
3. Niagara Apothecary
4. Prince of Wales Hotel
5. St. Vincent de Paul Parish Hall
6. St. Vincent de Paul Church
7. Shaw Festival Theatre
8. Niagara Hospital
9. Polish plot
10. St. Mark's Church
11. Parish Hall
12. Rectory
13. "Old Bank House"
14. Masonic Lodge No. 2

The restoration of the Court House needed about three years. In 1983 the huge vine was removed, revealing the attractive stonework, and all exterior repairs were carried out. The tower was removed, repaired, and replaced; the cupola, which had disappeared at some unknown date, was restored and beautifully lighted. The side entrance was improved to become the main entrance to the Court House Theatre. Close to it the elevator was installed, programmed to stop at five of the eight levels in the building.

The two halls were completed in time for the first Shaw play to open in late June 1984, and in September Parks Canada moved up from Navy Hall into offices on the left of the main corridor. Some basement space was found for library expansion, a Regional Police office, the Chamber of Commerce, and washrooms. Last of all the grounds were landscaped with walks and curbing, turf and ground planting.

The town now has a handsome, well-restored 1847 building with two major tenants, Parks Canada and the Shaw Festival. For its run of two or three months, the Shaw sets up its Court House Theatre, seating 350, in the large hall, and partitions off a third of the small hall for dressing-rooms. The rest of the year both halls are available for local purposes; indeed the charming restoration of those areas is fully visible only outside the theatre season.

Do read the two plaques in front of the Court House. The one headed "First Provincial Parliament, 1792" commemorates the meeting of the first legislature of the colony of Upper Canada (now Ontario), convened in this town by Lieutenant-Governor John Graves Simcoe. The other one, "Niagara Library, 1800" honours our long-established town library. Its entrance is around at the left side of the building.

Pause for a moment to admire the Clock Tower, erected as a memorial to those local boys who fell in the first Great War. Its clock controls the chimes for the hours and half-hours (which are also within the Court House), and it provides a pleasant focal point for our main street.

Across the road, on the corner to the right stands the Niagara Apothecary, Ontario's oldest drug store. Henry Paffard, a local druggist who was also the mayor, moved into the building in 1866; the business continued without interruption until it closed up shop in 1964. To save the building from demolition the Niagara Foundation purchased it, and the Ontario College of Pharmacy arranged for its restoration. Since 1971 it has been a museum, open in summer with free admission. Even when it is closed, however, you may press your nose against the windows to view the contents of a Confederation period pharmacy.

The author, conducting a visiting group on a walking tour in April 1985, pauses in front of the Niagara Apothecary.

Walk across King Street to continue along Picton with Simcoe Park on your left. This area was set aside in the earliest days of the town, and has been the scene of a tremendous variety of outdoor activities. The plaque to your left describes the formation of the Niagara Agricultural Society in 1792, which Lieutenant-Governor Simcoe assisted with his annual subscription of ten guineas. A similar plaque to your right, planted in the boulevard, gives a brief history of the town of Niagara; its status as the capital of Upper Canada for five years in Simcoe's time, its burning by the Americans in the War of 1812; and its position as seat for the District of Niagara till the 1860s.*

The original section of the Prince of Wales Hotel. A small wine shop occupies the corner of the building, and the hotel lobby is to the left in the recent addition.

On your right is the Prince of Wales Hotel, situated in a choice location at the main intersection in town. The oldest part is the three-storey section in the corner, built in the 1880s. No Prince of Wales ever stayed here; the hotel received its present name following the visit of the Duke and Duchess of Cornwall in 1901. Within the last ten years it has been skilfully expanded along King Street and Picton, while carefully retaining the 1836 Evans Cottage which you will see across the road.

As you approach the corner of Davy Street, look along it to notice the first building on the left away from the corner of Picton. This is the Parish Hall of St. Vincent de Paul Church; originally a gymnasium on the grounds of Camp Niagara, it was purchased at the end of World War II and moved here to fulfill a new role. The church itself, the oldest Roman Catholic Church in the Niagara Peninsula, comes into view as you approach the corner of Wellington. The original church (1835) is the rectangular part, and the round section nearer the street was added in 1965.

---

*On this plaque the date of the burning of Niagara is incorrectly given as December 13th. Both British and American commanders, however, reported that the town was burned on the 10th.

St. Vincent de Paul Church is rarely locked; do step inside for a quick visit. Notice that the earlier part of the building is marked off from the addition by a slab of grey stone left across the floor. The windows have been carefully matched for colour, but those in the original part have a more mellow tone. The loft for the organ and the choir has been cleverly designed to fit where the two sections of the church come together.

St. Vincent de Paul Roman Catholic Church as viewed across the cemetery. The 1835 section of the building blends in perfectly with the modern addition on the right.

As you leave St. Vincent de Paul, look diagonally across the corner for a view of the Shaw Festival Theatre. In the spring of 1973 this 867-seat theatre was completed, and was honoured by the attendance of Queen Elizabeth and Prince Philip at a performance of "You Never Can Tell" on June 28. Now turn left along Wellington. Across the road is the Niagara-on-the-Lake General Hospital, a forty-bed institution which is of real service to this community.

Many a visitor asks, "Do you have a by-law that says all houses here have to be built in an old style?" The answer is on the next corner--a tall house of unpainted wood, uniquely designed and imaginatively landscaped, but certainly ultra-modern in appearance. It complies with all the local building regulations, and is exactly what the owner planned for himself. By way of contrast, the house to its left has white stucco with black shutters, typical of many in this town.

At the corner turn left. Within a hundred metres you will see at the back of the Roman Catholic cemetery an area enclosed by a white wrought-iron fence. Within it are the graves of forty-one Polish soldiers who died in the 'flu epidemic of 1917 while training at Camp Niagara. "Why were they here?" you ask.

Near the end of World War I the Allies, having agreed on the principle of self-determination, decided that Poland deserved to be re-created as a nation when peace was restored. In order to have a military organization ready by that time, it was decided that a Polish force should be formed on a voluntary basis. At that moment, however, most of the men of Polish extraction who wished to join it were living in the U.S.A., which was still a neutral country. As a legal way around this situation, the Canadian government set aside a section of Camp Niagara to accommodate the Polish volunteers. Once the arrangement was known, a steady stream of them crossed the border as civilians to enrol here. During the next year and a half some 22,000 men received a month's basic training before passing on to other camps, eventually to serve in Poland itself.

Their stay in Niagara has not been forgotten. The middle Sunday of June is still observed as "Polish Sunday" in our town. From both sides of the border, but still mainly from the States, come citizens of Polish extraction, to hold a commemorative service at the Polish plot of St. Vincent de Paul. Speeches, hymns, banners--all are in Polish, but one theme of the occasion is the part that Camp Niagara and our little town played in the rebirth of their beloved homeland.

Now walk along the street almost to the corner, so that you can admire the fine Anglican rectory built in 1858 when Archdeacon William McMurray was commencing his ministry at St. Mark's Church. It is Italianate in style, the only house of its kind in the area, indicating the level of

prosperity of the church during that period. To the right of it
stands the Parish Hall, an 1886 building used on occasion
as a schoolhouse. The extensions on either side were
added in 1966 and eight windows were removed, leaving
interior archways. We shall see these windows in another
building in Tour 3; for now, observe the shape of those that
remain at the front of the Parish Hall.

St. Mark's Anglican Church and part of its old cemetery. The nearer section of the
church is the 1843 addition, and when that was completed the floor plan assumed
the shape of a cross.

To its right stands St. Mark's Anglican Church, with its
own cemetery. The first incumbent here was the Reverend
Robert Addison, sent out from England in 1792 as
"Missionary to Niagara" just before Lieutenant-Governor
and Mrs. Simcoe arrived here. The church itself was built
between 1804 and 1809, but all too soon had to be pressed
into use as a hospital when the War of 1812 began. The
Americans had no qualms about using the building when
they occupied the town during the following summer.
When they burned the town as they retreated across the
river on December 10 its wooden components went up in
flames, but the stone walls survived as a mere shell.

St. Mark's was rebuilt after the war, and enlarged in 1843
by the addition of the sanctuary and the transepts. Its
interior still retains a certain martial air: notice the number
of memorials on its walls to military men. Here is Colonel

John Butler, who formed the redoubtable Butler's Rangers during the American Revolution, officers who served and fell while defending Upper Canada during the War of 1812, and still others who died in service while their regiments were later posted here on garrison duty. Among them is the large memorial to William Kirby, an important townsman whom we shall meet again on two other tours.

On stepping out of St. Mark's, turn right to follow the driveway behind the church. On your right, close to the wall of the church which he helped to create, is the grave of Robert Addison, Some ten metres to its left lies a flat gravestone just above the turf. In 1813 when the Americans were occupying the town their army cooks used its flat surface as a convenient chopping-block on which to prepare meals for their soldiers at Fort George. The marks of their cleavers may still be seen if you look carefuly.

Returning to the driveway, follow it beyond the church until it reaches another driveway that comes from the street. Pause here to look left toward the river, and you will see a shallow indentation that winds its way downhill towards the back of the cemetery. This is what remains of a communication trench which the American soldiers dug during that summer. At the near end of the trench is a massive boulder, known as "Brock's Seat". According to local legend, it was originally on the shore, and was often used by Major-General Isaac Brock as a handy seat. In 1894, however, many years after Brock's death, the stone was in danger of being lost due to some change along the waterfront. William Kirby, who harboured strong feelings about history, had the stone moved and relocated right beside the American trench.

To recapture some of the spirit of those historic times, walk down that trench towards the back of the cemetery. Where it fades into the grass, go straight ahead and through the gate onto Ricardo Street. Turn left, and in half a block you are at the corner of King Street. Over to your right the Niagara River empties into Lake Ontario, and on the other side of it is New York State.

The solid-looking building to your left front bears the nameplate of the "Old Bank House". It was the local office of the Bank of Upper Canada a century and a half ago when

This memorial to Colonel John Butler, on the wall of St. Mark's, summarizes his career. The word "province" then meant "colony"; the war with France was the Seven Years' War; and the war of 1776 was the American Revolution, which the Americans call the War of Independence.

this part of town was the commercial area. Notice how the grassy verge on the east side of King Street widens out as it approaches Ricardo. This is where the railway tracks curved to the right as they came down King Street to cross Ricardo and descend to the Niagara wharf. The railway reached Niagara in 1855, connecting the town with Fort Erie, but the last train made its run just over a century later.

But let's not linger! We'll pass this way again on Tour 2, when we cover the waterfront. Turn left up King Street. The first court house and prison occupied about half the block on your right, starting at the corner of Prideaux. Like other buildings in town, it was damaged in the American bombardment that preceded the capture of the town. Now there's no hint of its location, for this block is filled with houses. After the War of 1812 the second court house was built (and it no longer exists either!) away out King Street, beyond the range of the guns of Fort Niagara.

As you approach the corner there is a good view of the Anglican rectory to your left. On the other side of Prideaux is the Masonic Hall, Lodge No. 2, a solid building with black shutters. This lodge was well-organized during Simcoe's governorship, and had its Freemasons' Hall at this location. The present building is believed to have been constructed from the rubble of the town after the war. It went through a variety of uses, but eventually was purchased by the Masons, who thus returned to the site of their original meetings.

As you pass the Masonic Lodge, notice the deep gulley on the other side of the road, in Simcoe Park. In the early days a sizable stream used to flow through here on its way to the lake. Much later it proved a convenient place for a large skating rink, until the artificial ice of the Virgil Arena became available in 1967.

A walk of one block, past a fascinating variety of houses, brings you back to the Niagara Apothecary, and so back to the car park.

ALONG THE WATERFRONT

This is an exciting tour in various ways. The early exploration of this part of North America proceeded along its waterways, especially the Great Lakes system. In the clash of empires, this area was always of military importance; forts were built here, and we shall see three of them. Early settlement began along the Niagara River, and our town grew up beside it. From the first the river was a highway to the interior, and if Niagara Falls presented an obstacle to that travel, it soon excited men's imagination and attracted visitors then, just as it still does. In that travel the railroad and the steamers, both of which came to our town, played their part for many years.

In two respects this waterfront tour is a long one. Chronologically it covers about three centuries, right up to an event of last year and a problem for the future. Its total length is more than most of the others, therefore it has been divided into two parts, both of which begin and end at Queen's Royal Park. That's a convenient place to leave your car, for it has no parking meters, but it does have washrooms!

UPSTREAM: THE EARLY DAYS
(15 blocks)

Begin by going up onto the ridge that overlooks the water. Here the Niagara River, flowing north, empties into Lake Ontario in front of you. To the right, upstream nineteen kilometres, is Niagara Falls; Fort Erie and Buffalo, about fifty. If it's a reasonably clear day, a long look to your left across the lake may reveal the downtown Toronto skyline. On the far side of the river is the U.S.A., and this section of it is part of New York State.

On the American shore at the extreme left stands Fort Niagara. This is easily the oldest building on either side of the border in this whole area. The original wooden fort on that site was built there by the decision of the explorer La Salle. This one, often called the "French Castle" because of its appearance, was constructed by the French in 1726 with the permission of the Senecas, ostensibly as a post for trading. During the Seven Years' War it was besieged and captured by the British two months before General Wolfe's expedition took Quebec. Britain, recognizing its strategic value, strengthened it by the addition of two redoubts, of which the pagoda-like roof of one is visible from here.

A view of old Fort Niagara from Queen's Royal Park. On the point is the French "castle", with the low bakehouse beside it. One of the British-built redoubts is visible. In the trees to the right are three flags: the fleur-de-lys, the Union Jack, and in the centre, the Stars and Stripes.

During the American Revolution Fort Niagara became a place of safety for those in the Thirteen Colonies who wished to remain loyal to King George III. Refugees from the frontier regions of New York, Pennsylvania, New Jersey, and further south, as well as Indians of the Six Nations whose crops and villages had been burned by the

Americans, fled there to place themselves under the protection of the British garrison. At Fort Niagara the colonial regiment known as Butler's Rangers was formed in 1777, and it was from that fort that many of the United Empire Loyalists crossed the river to take up land once more under the British flag.

The British garrison remained at Fort Niagara even after the treaty of peace was signed with the Americans. By the time they withdrew across the river in 1796, Britain, about to give up a valuable base, had begun the construction of Fort George on this side. Old Fort Niagara is unique in that it was built by the French, added to by the British, and later, at the time of the Civil War, by the Americans also.

To the right of Queen's Royal Park are two streets; take the upper one, which is Ricardo. In the first block it runs behind St. Mark's cemetery. Notice on the left side two houses, numbers 45 and 47, whose adjacent walls come together. These were obviously built by a couple of good neighbours in the days before building regulations forbade such chumminess.

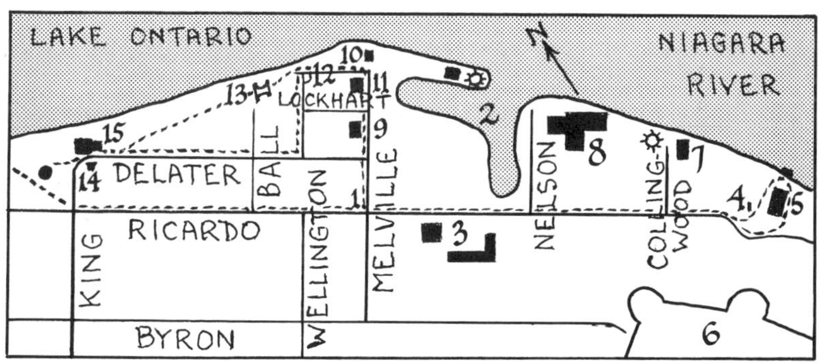

Tour 2 - Upstream

1. Butler's Barracks site	6. Fort George	12. Locomotive
2. Marina	7. Waterworks	turntable
3. The Anchorage	8. "Old Boat Works"	13. Old culvert
Motor Hotel	9. George III Hotel	14. Horse-trough
4. Simcoe Monument	10. Immigration office	15. Whale Inn
5. Navy Hall	11. Harbour Inn	☼ Lighthouse

In the corner at the end of the block, on an elevation to the right sits a pleasant red-brick house in the trees, with a gazebo close to the corner of the lot. A few years after the Civil War the owner of this house had a brief visit from

Jefferson Davis, who had been president of the Confederate States. Davis was kindly received in Niagara, and later in Toronto; he commented that he felt more at home on this side of the border than in the northern U.S.A.

At the next corner, Melville Street, a triangular plot of land has been fenced off and graced with an historic plaque. This marks the site of Butler's Barracks, built during the winter of 1778-9. Its construction was authorized by Governor Haldimand to alleviate the overcrowding at Fort Niagara, but when the bill was rendered he complained about the high expenditure for rum while the Rangers laboured at their task. When they moved into these barracks, it is likely that some brought their wives and families with them, and these may have been the first, though unrecorded, settlers on this side of the river.

Once the American Revolution drew to a close and the Rangers were disbanded, their barracks were put to a variety of uses in the years that followed. When the War of 1812 came along, however, these buildings were exposed to the American bombardment preceding the capture of the town, and it seemed futile to maintain them any longer. They were replaced by a second set of barracks buildings which we shall visit in Tour 7.

From here go straight ahead on Ricardo Street, pausing to admire the marina on your left and the Anchorage, a favourite hostelry for the sailing crowd, on your right. A long block further on, keep to the left of the circular flowerbed in the road, and pause to read the historic plaque close to it. This gives a brief biography of John Graves Simcoe, first Lieutenant-Governor of Upper Canada. Now pass through the wrought-iron gates, and there before you is a handsome memorial to the Governor and Mrs. Simcoe, erected by the Niagara Parks Commission in 1952. The book in her hand is a reminder that it is chiefly through her diary, written for their young daughters left behind in England, that we have a picture of social life in Upper Canada in the 1790s.

Pass to the left of Navy Hall and go down to the small wharf beside it. Away to your left old Fort Niagara is visible past the willow tree; across the river, stretching upstream to your right, is Youngstown, N.Y. You are now on the spot where Governor Simcoe and his party stepped ashore from the "Onondaga" on 26 July 1792, after a voyage from Kingston that took **three days** because of adverse winds.

There was already a group of four wooden buildings on this site. Erected before the American Revolution for the use of the Provincial Marine, they were labelled on early maps as "Navy Hall". The Simcoes had expected to occupy one of these buildings, but finding it not ready they made their home in three marquees pitched at the top of the hill. During the five years that Newark (as Simcoe re-named Niagara) was the capital of the colony the buildings of Navy Hall saw a great deal of use. The Simcoes eventually lived in one of them, and one or more were probably used for some sessions of the legislature.

Navy Hall, abandoned and half-forgotten, as it looked early this century.

After York (now Toronto) became the capital of Upper Canada and the centre of activity moved further from the water, the buildings fell into disuse, till only one remained. Even that nearly perished: it was twice shifted a few yards, once to avoid a railway siding; for a time it was used as a stable, till the Niagara Historical Society took up the cudgels on its behalf. During World War I it was repaired to become the inoculation centre for Camp Niagara, then it was abandoned once more.

Finally in 1930 the Ontario government undertook to rescue the building. It was repaired with old wood, perhaps salvaged from other buildings, and encased in stone. The Navy Hall that you see today may not be on its original site, and it was **not** a stone building in the first place. Nevertheless it is one of the few remaining links with the early days of Upper Canada. Some years ago it contained a museum, then it housed the Parks Canada offices until they moved into the main floor of the Court House in 1984. It is planned to make Navy Hall a museum again sometime in the future.

From the wharf continue round Navy Hall to view Fort George from below. By Jay's Treaty of 1794 Britain agreed to give up Fort Niagara; this she did two years later, thereby ending what the Americans refer to as the "holdover period". Governor Simcoe ordered that Fort George be built as a replacement. It was a large fort with six bastions, designed as a supply depot and headquarters for the forts on the upper lakes, rather than a stronghold to be defended. At the time, of course, it seemed that Britain and the States, having settled their various differences, had begun a period of prolonged friendship.

That expectation was rudely terminated when the U.S.A. declared war in June 1812. On May 27 the following year, Fort George, badly battered in the preliminary bombardment, was captured by the Americans. They occupied our town all that summer, and when they retreated across the river on December 10, their commander ordered that the town be put to the torch. The houses of Niagara were soon rebuilt, but Fort George lay in such a damaged state that

Powder Magazine, Fort George

it was abandoned in the 1820s, and sank into decay for over a century.

The restoration of Fort George was undertaken in 1937 as a make-work project of the depression, through the co-operation of the federal government and the Niagara Parks Commission. The task was completed three years later, and the fort has grown to be a major attraction of this town. The tour of Fort George requires about an hour, and we suggest you find time for this as a separate outing.

As you go back along Ricardo, notice Collingwood, a short street that leads towards the river. The red-brick building at the end of it is the waterworks, constructed in 1891. This was built to supply the town with water from the Niagara River, and in its first years with electric power also. Lately there has been serious concern about the pollution of the river, with the result that Town Council secured a safer water supply from DeCew Falls beginning on 18 August 1982. Some discussion has taken place regarding possible use of the waterworks building as a maritime museum.

The next complex of buildings on your right was developed by Shepherd's Boats, which began here in 1939 and launched many a fine vessel over the years. It was later bought out by Trojan, and then by Whittaker, which closed the plant in 1978. Since that time the main building was used as an office during 1980, the one summer when the hydrofoil connected the town with Toronto, but its last activity was to house a flea market. The forlorn yacht which stands beside the entrance seems to indicate the uncertain future of "The Old Boat Works".

The marina, by contrast, is a hive of activity. Originally a mosquito-infested riverside marsh, the area was bought and developed by the Niagara Harbour and Dock Company in 1831. During the flourishing days of Niagara in the 1840s this was the chief industry in town, employing as many as 350 hands to turn out sailboats, steamers, barges, and steam-engines as required. Eventually the shipbuilding business migrated to the vicinity of the Welland Canal, but today the marina, operated since 1979 by the Niagara-on-the-Lake Sailing Club, continues as one of the chief attractions of old Niagara.

Several services that support the marina are located in this area. On the lower side of Ricardo Street is the large building that houses Murray's Boat Repairs. A new boat-launching ramp has been built on the nearer edge of the Old Boat Works property, with access from Nelson Street.

Now turn down Melville Street. At the bottom of the grade stands an hotel known as the "American" for many years; a few years ago the new owners re-named it the "George III", thereby reversing the outcome of the American Revolution. Across the road are the entrances to the marina, and further down the street are the immigration office and the dock, with the lighthouse and the store to the right.

In years gone by Niagara was both a destination and a major transfer point in the trip between Toronto and Buffalo. The steamers--and earlier this century there were three of them making daily runs--used to tie up at this dock. At the other side of it stood the ticket office and freight shed for the railway, which ran via Niagara Falls to Fort Erie and Buffalo. From this dock the local farmers could despatch their fruit, and commercial fishermen their catch, in either direction The last of the steamers, the well-loved "Cayuga", made its final run in 1957, and the trains ceased coming down to the wharf.

Reel for Drying Fish Net

On this reel Ted Ball, our last commmercial fisherman, used to dry his gill-nets. It stands where the O in "Lockhart" appears on the map on page 15. Ted last fished in the 1978 season, and he died in 1986.

There still remain two visible pieces of evidence that the railway line once came here. Turn left at the white immigration shed, and go past the Harbour Inn to the next corner. By the road surface on the near left corner is a large

The Niagara dock, as viewed from a steamer early this century. Note the railway carriages waiting to the right of the ticket office and freight shed.

The "Cayuga" at the Niagara dock. Though its last trip across the lake was made in 1957, some visitors still recall with pleasure their outings on this steamer.

chunk of masonry that continues in a circular pattern till it returns to disappear under the road. This was the base for the turntable for the locomotive.

After the railway ceased to run, the turntable was filled in and its 55-foot circle became overgrown. In 1988 the historical society managed to have the remaining railway lands and the turntable historically designated. On June 28 a group of enthusiastic volunteers turned out to clear up the untidy site, uncovering the locomotive turntable for all to see.

Now look ahead in line with the river. Fifty yards on is a shaggy hump overgrown with weeds. If you examine this you will find that it hides a stone culvert. The top of this indicates the level of the railway embankment as the line descended to the Niagara wharf.

At this point there are two ways to go. You may walk straight ahead, over the culvert, and along the grassy right-of-way near the water. If you prefer the road, turn left, and after two short blocks, turn right onto Delater Street.

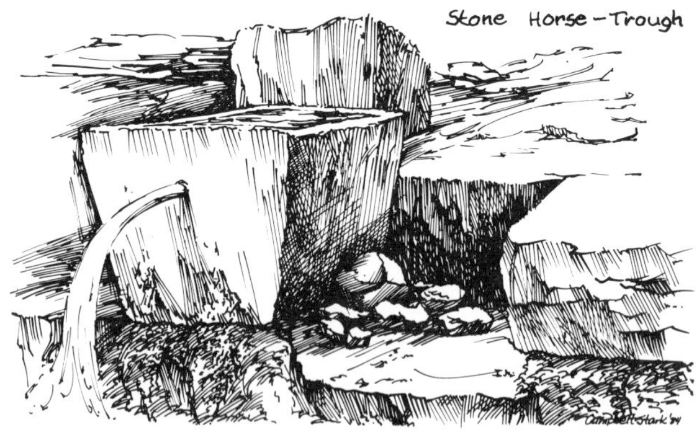

Either of these routes brings you to the end of Delater Street, where the road rises and bends to the left onto King Street. Near this corner look for the heavy stone horse-trough on the left. A few years ago the little stream flowed down the hill and filled it with water that poured gaily from the hole in the front, providing a constant drinking fountain. Now it is earth-filled, and the stream flows alongside. Dull, eh?

About here the railway line, descending from King Street on its way to the dock, used to run behind the white Edwardian bungalow on the left, and over Delater on a trestle bridge. The massive stone blocks alongside the horse-trough remain from that place of engineering.

The large house on the right is the Whale Inn, built about 1835. The wing at the lower level was particularly convenient for sailors when it was originally a tavern; the

The Whale Inn, built in the 1830s. Notice the fire insurance sign over the door (see page 41). The low marker in the foreground indicates the site of the Niagara "Gleaner".

traveller could beach his craft on the shore, order a dram as he walked in, and warm himself at the big open fireplace. For many years this was a thriving boardinghouse, but now, tastefully restored, it is a private residence.

In the days when the Whale Inn was new, this immediate area must have been a centre of activity, as indicated by the historical plaque and the Niagara Historical Society marker. The first newspaper, the "Upper Canada Gazette and American Oracle", was published in 1792 in a building on King Street, and after the War of 1812 the "Gleaner" had a twenty-year run on the same site. The Royal Engineers' quarters occupied a building close to the water, in line with the street. These buildings vanished long ago, and now it is a pleasant park. By the way, isn't it time for lunch?

DOWNSTREAM: TO THE PRESENT

(11 blocks)

In this park there once stood the most prestigious hotel in Niagara, the Queen's Royal. It was a four-storey white bulding with green shutters, occupying the high ground overlooking the river. The level grassy area next to King Street was once the bowling green, and the tennis court fitted in where the cars are parked. At the far end a casino or dance pavilion extended from the main building; a walkway went past it near the water's edge to the clubhouse of the golf course.

The hotel was built because of a political decision. When the county replaced the district as the operative unit for municipal government, St. Catharines was selected as the seat for Lincoln County in preference to the older town of Niagara. Our town fathers protested to the government of the United Canadas to such good effect that $8,000 was paid to Niagara as compensation. With these funds our council built an hotel on this site in 1869. It shortly passed into private hands, and before the end of the Victorian period the Queen's Royal had become a summer holiday mecca for tourists from both sides of the border.

A view of the Queen's Royal Hotel from a steamer, around 1900.

It had much to offer. From a wicker chair or rocker on its broad verandah the visitor could survey the water, admiring the graceful sailboats, the scheduled arrivals and departures of the Toronto steamers, and the local fishermen toiling at their nets or lines. On the beach below, the bathers paddled or swam, and there were rowboats for hire. It was a high-class hotel: the old guest registers indicate that its patrons were often accompanied by a servant or a nursemaid for the children. Here the Duke and Duchess of Cornwall (later King George V and Queen Mary) spent a few days in 1901. For the town the Queen's Royal was a considerable benefit through the various kinds of employment that it generated.

The hotel began to experience hard times when the family automobile became more common. Eventually it closed its doors, the contents were sold, and it was dismantled during the depression. The town retained the property, developing it gradually into a picnic area, and naming the park after the elegant hotel which once stood there. During the past few years, as more visitors began to come to town, its grounds have been landscaped, trees have been planted, the shoreline has been protected with a breakwater after the destructive erosion of 1973, and washrooms were added six years later.

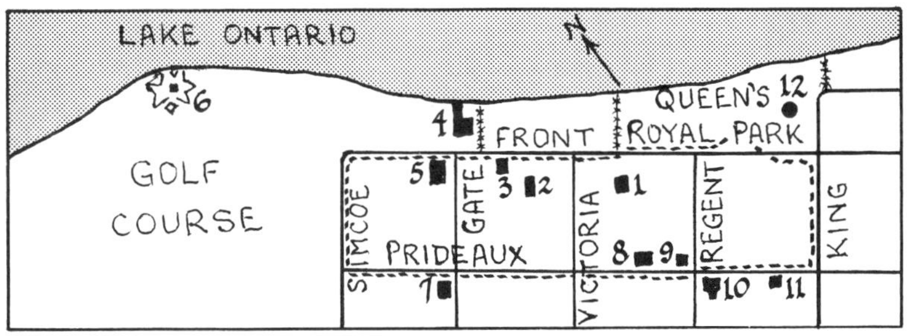

Tour 2 - Downstream

1. Captain's House
2. Delatre Lodge
3. William Kirby's house
4. Clubhouse for golf course
5. Oban Inn
6. Fort Mississauga
7. 155 Gate Street
8. "Demeath"
9. Promenade House
10. Stewart-McLeod house
11. McKee house
12. "Dead Zone" gazebo

From Queen's Royal Park continue along Front Street. On the left the "Captain's House" occupies an elevated site. This was built in the 1820s for Captain Edward Oates, skipper of the packet "Duke of Richmond"; from its verandah his wife could watch for his vessel as it approached Niagara. In the next block is "Delatre Lodge", somewhat like it in appearance, which acquired its name from Colonel Philip Delatre*, who was for a time president of the Harbour and Dock Company. Next door, marked with an historic plaque, is the home of William Kirby, a prominent citizen who edited the Niagara "Mail" for many years, then served as customs collector for Niagara. Kirby was also a literary figure whose best-known work was "The Golden Dog", a Victorian novel about the final years of New France. When the Royal Society of Canada was formed in 1882, he was elected as one of its Fellows.

This picture was taken from Fort Mississauga during World War I, looking back along what is now No. 1 hole of the golf course. Note Brock's Monument on the skyline near the left.

Just ahead stands the clubhouse of the Niagara Golf Club, overlooking the mouth of the river. This nine-hole course was set up early this century, but when World War I broke out the club was forced to vacate so that the area could be used as an extension of Camp Niagara. Returning by 1920, the club has developed a well-manicured course that is an additional attraction for our town.

Across the road is the Oban Inn, a long-established hotel, of which the original part was built as the home of another steamer captain, Duncan Milloy, sometime after the War of 1812. It has been added to over the years, and during World War I it housed the officers' mess for those troops that occupied the golf course. As you proceed along Front Street, look to the right to enjoy another view of Fort Niagara. Here the club has had the trees along the river

---

* The street mentioned on page 22 was named after Colonel Delatre because of his connection with that company. At some unknown date the local council anglicized the street name, spelling it as "Delater".

bank trimmed back so as to provide a fine panorama for the diners at the Oban.

At the corner of Simcoe Street, look ahead some three hundred metres for a view of Fort Mississauga. It was constructed largely as a reaction to the American capture of Fort George. The central tower rose rapidly in 1814, using the bricks of the lighthouse that stood on that spot, and the gaunt chimneys that were all that remained of some houses in the town. The Treaty of Ghent ended the war before the year was out, consequently other work on the log huts and earthworks of the new fort proceeded very slowly.

When Fort George itself was abandoned in the 1820s, Butler's Barracks on the Commons became the military headquarters. The British garrison stationed there sent detachments to man Fort Mississauga, but according to one observer this duty was not taken seriously. Anna Jameson, passing this way early in 1837, described it:

"The Americans have a fort on their side, and we also have a fort on ours. What the amount of their garrison may be I know not, but our force consists of three privates and a corporal, with adequate arms and ammunition, i.e. rusty firelocks and damaged guns. The fortress itself I mistook for a dilapidated brewery. This is charming -- it looks like peace and security, at all events."

The Oban, as viewed from the #1 tee of the golf course. From its upper verandah and from the diningroom on the near side there is a fine view of the lake and Fort Niagara.

However, when the Mackenzie rebellion occurred later that year and its leader fled to the U.S.A., Fort Mississauga was fully manned, and it was strengthened in the 1840s. During the Civil War it was again kept in a state of readiness, but by 1870 Britain had withdrawn the garrison altogether. After that the fort was allowed to decay, though a coat of parging was applied to protect the tower from the weather. The huts fell down, erosion carried away part of the earthworks, and the area became a useful cow pasture.

When the golf club leased the land, the fort was worked into the course without difficulty. Two tees were located on top of the earthworks, and the green for the 185-yard number 2 hole was cunningly placed close to the tower, providing the golfers with a unique conversation piece.

In 1976 Parks Canada proposed a plan to restore Fort Mississauga and open the area to visitors. Local citizens, whether golfers or not, generally rallied to the support of the golf club, and Parks Canada had to be content with a partial victory. The green and the two tees have been moved away from the fort; the tower has been stabilized by repairing the brickwork and removing the loose parging. The golf club has now a lease that runs to 1990, and it is likely that this will be renewed.

Fort Mississauga, after its stabilization by Parks Canada. To the left of the tower is the gate, flanked by the two ammunition bays; to the right is the sally-port.

Fort Mississauga, unlike its two neighbours, has never been tested in battle. The only missiles that have struck its tower were the golf-balls once aimed at the second green.

If you want to see it at close quarters, slip out there early in the morning before the golfers are about, and look for:
   -two historic plaques, about the lighthouse and the fort
   -the ammunition bays and the sally-port
   -traces of the log huts within the earthworks
   -a view of Fort Niagara, perhaps even Toronto
   -trace of a World War I trench west of the earthworks

But enough of the military; the rest is residential. Go left on Simcoe, and left again onto Prideaux. At the end of the first block, look carefully at the large buff-coloured house on the right, 155 Gate Street. This was originally the Methodist meeting-house, constructed in the 1820s on their property three blocks further up Gate. Later it was sold and moved to the present site. One would never guess by its appearance that it was a place of worship a century ago.

In the next block, as in the first, the houses are chiefly interesting because of their different designs and ages. In the third block there are two small houses on the left, close to the street line, that were probably built by John Davidson, the skilled joiner who made the pulpit and sounding-board for St. Andrew's Church. The large brick house next door but one, "Demeath", was built right after the War of 1812 on the foundation of an earlier one. It was the home of Dr. Robert Kerr, a respected citizen, surgeon to the Indian Department, who was married to Elizabeth, a daughter of Molly Brant and Sir William Johnson. It is thought that he had his office in this house, with an entrance from the street; a scrutiny of the four lower windows will suggest which one was originally the doorway to it.

At the end of the block, on the left stands the brick Promenade House, built about 1820. It was an hotel in Victorian times, accommodating some of its guests in a long wooden annex that extended down Regent Street. That has long disappeared; the house has been a private residence for many years, and the brown wrap-around addition is quite recent.

Diagonally across the street is the Stewart-McLeod, house, built for a local lawyer a few years later. Notice the fine detail of the doorway, and the arcaded arches of the upper windows. As originally constructed, the house was

This fine house belonged to Dr. Robert Kerr. It stands on a double lot, extending all the way back to Front Street.

The Stewart-McLeod house is a typical Georgian house, with its centre entrance and symmetrical appearance.

somewhat pretentious, for it was only one room deep; the wing at the back and the ornamental picket fence are both additions by the present owner. Nevertheless, it contains one of the finest spiral staircases of that period.*

*A picture of that staircase appears in "The Ancestral Roof" by MacRae and Adamson (1963) on page 53.

By way of contrast, the tall house across the road is hardly ten years old. Those in the rest of the block present an interesting mixture. On the left, for example, is a two-storey house with a mansard roof, the garage styled to match the house itself. Across the street is another old house so close to the sidewalk that the front steps rise parallel to it. The simple clapboard house (c. 1835) two further along is similarly placed, but is unusual in that the gable end faces the street and the entrance is on the side. Notice the lower windows with their small panes, twelve over eight. (How would you like to clean them, or paint their woodwork?)

The house across the road underwent an ingenious remodelling a few years ago. The owners, who lived in the large house on the corner, always referred to it as their "cottage". The term suited, for it was a narrow little house with a double garage to the right. In the renovation they sacrificed one side of the garage, to increase the frontage of the cottage by half and to add a walkway to the back garden. The upper storey was re-shaped to provide for three flat dormers. The join between the original structure and the addition is hidden behind the right-hand downpipe. The result is eminently satisfactory: a little old house preserved, enlarged, and sporting a new name-plate, "Burberry Cottage".

From here turn left onto King Street, which will take you back to Queen's Royal Park. To bring this tour to a suitable conclusion, go and stand for a moment in the green-roofed gazebo (or is it a bandshell?) that sits on the grassy slope not far from the water. This is the newest public building in town, constructed in January 1983 for the filming of some scenes in the movie "The Dead Zone". Director David Cronenberg secured permission to have it built, and to use several other locations in town, in order to simulate the New Hampshire town in which some of the action took place. For a few weeks our quiet Niagara winter was enlivened with new visitors and a taste of movie-making. The townspeople seem pleased to have the gazebo: it adds a pleasant touch to the park, it cost us no tax money, and nobody has objected to the American eagle surmounting it.

The gazebo has already undergone some changes. The next spring our town council had the metal roof covered with split cedar shingles. Then, one dark night in August, persons unknown piled up picnic benches on the near side and made off with the eagle. In the summer of 1988, however, local craftsman Jim Smith designed and installed the present sailing-ship weathervane.

Queen's Royal Park also attracts tourists of another type. The ridge where the hotel once stood is an ideal spot for bird-watching, especially during the annual migration. On any weekend the warmly-clad birdwatchers may be seen there, scanning the river with binoculars and telescopes, hoping to add a few species to their life lists.

Now look over at Fort Niagara, not the whole complex but the original French castle. The fort and the gazebo are separated by about seven hundred metres of water, and by two-and-a-half centuries of history. In all the major events of that period of time the town of Niagara has had a part.

FOR MUSEUM BUFFS

(6 blocks)

This tour, though relatively short, will take you past two school buildings now put to other uses, and two museums. If the museums are open and you decide to visit them, the walk will take longer than the distance would indicate. On the other hand, once you know where they are located, you might wish to return at another time to do them thoroughly.

Leave your car in the parking lot behind the Court House, and come out onto King Street, turning right. The first building you pass is a one-storey white clapboard house. This was the station for the electric railway that joined Niagara to St. Catharines in 1913. Tickets were sold inside, but the generous overhang of the eaves was made for the benefit of the customers while they waited for the streetcar. The line ran along the near side of King Street, bearing to the right where it left town. The trolley made its last run in 1931, defeated by the depression and the proliferation of the family automobile.

Just past the next house stands the fire hall for the old town. This took shape in the summer of 1964, replacing the one that was around the corner on Queen Street (see page 49). It was not a new building then; for many years it had been the premises of Jack Greene's livery stable. The firemen, many of whom were experienced craftsmen, contributed seven thousand man-hours of free work to modify the building to its new use.

The town volunteer fire department has a long and distinguished history. It was formed in 1816, when the burning of the town by the Americans was fresh in everyone's memory, and it was incorporated ten years later. At one period there were two rival organizations--the Hook and Ladder Company and the Hose Company--but later they got together, though some rivalry continues in a friendly way between A Company and B Company. They meet regularly through the winter for training on Monday evening, but at any hour of the day or night the sound of the fire siren will bring our firemen from all quarters to man their equipment and dash to the scene of the fire.

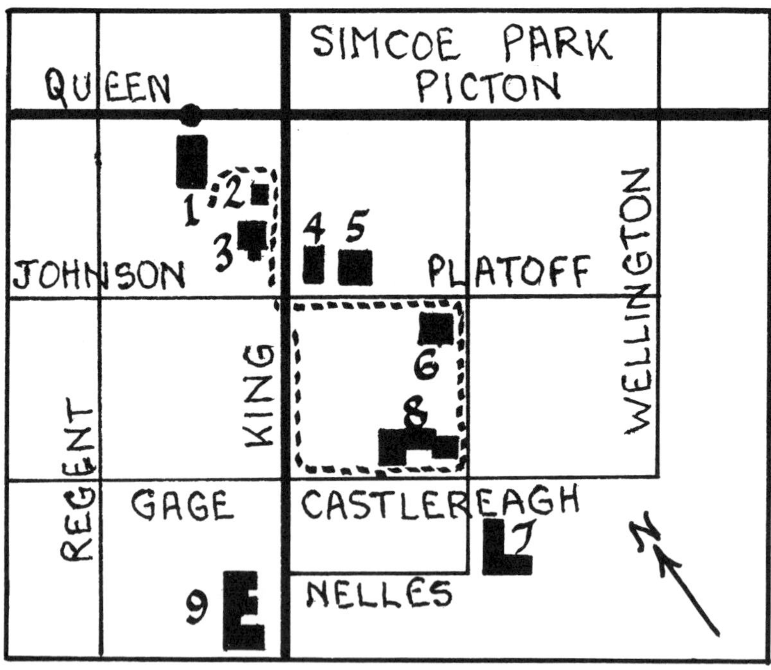

Tour 3

1. Court House
2. Electric railway station (former)
3. Fire Hall and Museum
4. Moore-Bishop-Stokes house
5. Community Hall
6. Public School (former)
7. Simcoe Hall
8. Niagara Historical Society Museum
9. Parliament Oak Public School

Attached to the left side of the fire hall is the Fire Museum. The building is a new one, constructed by the firemen themselves during 1971-2. There you will see pieces of old equipment from the local scene, as well as items donated by other fire departments that have no museum of their own. Though it is open only during the summer, it is well worth a visit. It is also under the management of the Niagara Historical Society.

Across the road and on the corner is the home of a well-known restoration architect and his wife. When they purchased the house, built about 1828, it was a nondescript building, clad in blue-grey insulbrick. Today a pleasant yellow, it has been restored inside and out, and improved in appearance by the addition of the bay window to the left of the front door.

Now turn left onto Platoff Street. A few years ago the building on the left used to be a part of Arkell Industries; the back part of that canning factory was taken down, enlarging the Prince of Wales parking lot, and the front part was refurbished to become the town Community Centre.

The two houses across the street--the two-storey number 16 and the board-and-batten cottage at number 20--were both built about 1840, when the old town's population was greater than it is right now. For another one of the same vintage, look to your left when you reach the corner; the large house at 230 Davy Street has a complete front verandah with French windows looking out onto it, and elaborate "gingerbread" under the porch eaves.

The large brick building at the right was built in 1859 as the town public school. It started out with four classrooms, with each teacher, including the principal, responsible for two grades. Go round the corner onto Davy to see two buildings added later behind the school. The first was a low white building that held the washrooms; today, with a small addition, it has become a house. The next one along Davy Street was built to take care of the Primer (or Grade 1), in the days before kindergartens were established, and it too has become a residence. The school served until 1948, when Parliament Oak Public School was built on King Street. The school site was then sold, the brick school-house divided into apartments, and the other two buildings made into houses.

Fourth room class in front of Niagara Public School, 1921. Note the attractive fanlight over the doorway. (Townspeople! Can you identify Bert Hall, Nixon Brennan, and Ted Bradley?)

On the next corner, Castlereagh Street, the newish two-storey building away from the centre of town is Simcoe Hall, apartments for senior citizens. The corner to your right is occupied by the Niagara Historical Society Museum, whose development is a story in itself.

In the early days of Upper Canada the legislature passed a law to establish grammar schools at four centres in the colony, including Niagara. For a long time the Niagara Grammar School met in various places in town, but finally in 1875 a two-roomed schoolhouse was erected.

Notice the date above the front door, which now faces out onto the lawn. In 1908 the Grammar School celebrated its one hundredth anniversary with considerable pride. A couple of years later two more rooms were added, and a small gymnasium, extending it to the right and around the corner onto Davy Street.

In the meantime a group of fifteen citizens had formed the Niagara Historical Society in 1895. It embarked on an active programme, holding meetings, collecting artifacts, and publishing pamphlets about the early days of Niagara. To hold its growing collection, the society built the Memorial Hall in 1907; that is the tall building with the portico, over to your left. (This, by the way, was five years before the Royal Ontario Museum opened in Toronto.)

Soon after World War II the decision was made to bus the local secondary school students to Stamford Collegiate in Niagara Falls, and our high school was closed. Town council disposed of the school site: the gymnasium on Davy Street was sold to two local doctors and severed from the rest of the building, to provide a driveway between; the remaining part, fronting on Castlereagh, was turned over to the historical society as an annex.

For some years the society operated its museum in two buildings, the Memorial Hall and most of the old high school. When the federal government began its Local

Niagara Historical Society Museum. The original Memorial Hall is on the left, and the old high school on the right was later acquired as an annex. The bridging section in the centre connected the two in 1973.

Initiatives Programme, however, the society secured a grant to construct a bridging section connecting the two, and this was opened in June 1973. One unusual feature: the eight windows which had been part of the original St. Mark's Parish Hall, and which were removed when it was enlarged (see page 9) were now taken out of storage and installed in the new section of the museum!

As you can see, this museum is of unusual shape, and its three parts are all of different ages. Though it receives provincial and municipal grants each year, the Niagara Historical Society Museum is one of the few in Ontario which is still managed by the executive of the society which built it. Of late years the society has been able to employ a permanent curator, so that with some voluntary help its museum is open practically every day of the year. Its collection numbers some twenty thousand artifacts, many of them dating back to the War of 1812 and the time of the United Empire Loyalists. An hour or so in browsing through it is time well spent.

The homes in the area across from the museum and on the near side of King Street are easily recognizable as World War II housing. In some communities such an area would have deteriorated, but in Niagara these houses have been well maintained, and in some cases enlarged, so that they are good for many more years.

From the museum proceed along Castlereagh to King Street. At the corner you will see on your left Parliament Oak Public School, which replaced the one we saw earlier. Turn right onto King Street, and a walk of two blocks will bring you back to the corner where we started.

This tour would not be complete without a comment on a characteristic of Niagara that you may already have noticed. We rarely discard anything, whether it's a building or just part of one; we just wait until an opportunity to recycle it turns up. You will see other examples of this thrifty habit in later tours.

SCOTS WHA HA'E
(18 blocks)

This time our route will take us through a residential area, passing a number of houses of various ages and designs. One church is included, St. Andrew's Presbyterian, hence the title for this outing. Assuming that you've parked your car behind the Court House, walk out onto King Street, turn right for one block, then right again onto Johnson Street.

No two of the houses in the old town are alike, and their distance from the street line varies depending on the date of construction. On the left, for example, Walnut Cottage is close to the sidewalk; the next two are well back, but the style of their porches is quite different. Across the road we come to the bowling green at the corner of Regent. The club claims to have been formed about a century ago; it moved here from the grounds of the Queen's Royal when that great hotel vanished. Looking above the bowling green, we have a good view of the back of the Court House.

On the corner to our left are two fine old houses, both facing Johnson. The nearer one, Barker Hall, has been divided into apartments and clad in asbestos shingles--but note the fine doorcase, a clue to its original grandeur. On the other corner the Eckersley house is a single-family dwelling. Its chimneys are placed, not on the exterior walls, but well into the building, providing corner fireplaces for some rooms. It too has a well-designed doorway.

Next comes a house hardly ten years old, an example of local in-filling. Two further on, the one-storey house well back from the street used to be a garage not many years ago. Across the road are houses that have been renovated and painted in interesting colours.

At the corner of Victoria the Vanderlip-Marcy house on the left at 96 Johnson is well-preserved, with open fireplaces, pine floors, and corner cupboards. At one time it had a small front porch, but when the sidewalk was put down it had to be removed. Rather than being destroyed, it was moved a block or so and installed on another house.

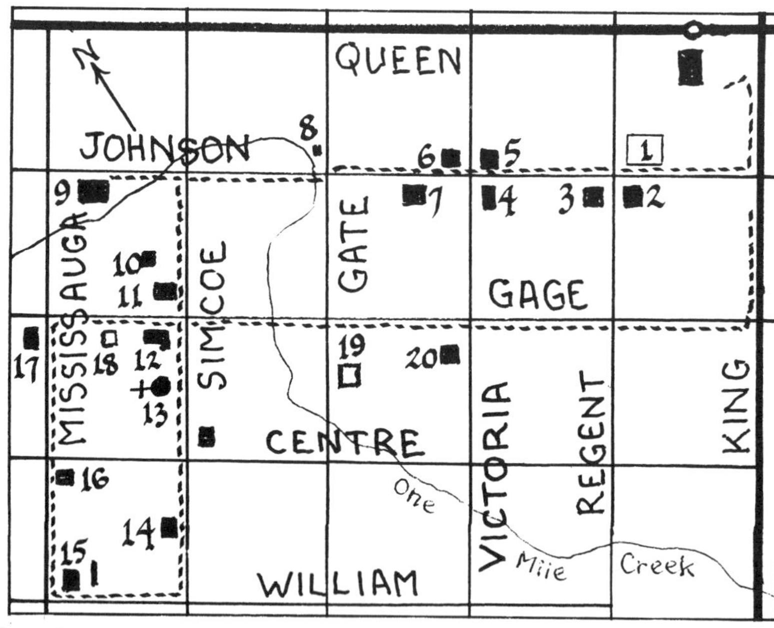

Tour 4

1. Bowling green
2. Barker Hall
3. Eckersley house
4. Vanderlip-Marcy house
5. Blain-Lansing house
6. Hendrie house
7. Crown Hotel
8. "Slave Cottage"
9. Clench house
10. Johnson house
11. Lockhart-Moogk house
12. St. Andrew's Kirk Hall
13. St. Andrew's Church
14. Creen house
15. Breakenridge-Hawley house
16. Breakenridge-Ure house
17. Camp-Thompson house
18. Presbyterian meeting-house site
19. Methodist cemetery
20. Carlisle-Brook house

Across the road stands the brick Blain-Lansing house, whose date of construction (1845) may be seen in the keystone above the doorway. Many years ago the postmaster lived there, and it is believed that an entrance to the office was provided on the corner of the building. When this was filled in, the bricks did not quite match, and the difference is still visible.

On the third corner is the Hendrie house, a large well-kept two-storey dwelling with a lean-to addition. When we came to town it was a double, but recent owners have restored and repainted, adding a plaque for identification.

The fourth corner once had one of the two houses which were supposed to have survived the burning of the town by the Americans in December of 1813. Eventually it became so decrepit that it had to be taken down. The other of those two houses, which stood three blocks away, had already perished, with the result that there are today no houses in the old town that pre-date the War of 1812.

In the next block your eye will at once be attracted to the three red houses with curved handrails beside the front steps. These were built about 1840 as humble workers' houses; today they are combined to accommodate two families. The large white house across the road was once the Crown Hotel. Note the black oval above the front door. This is an old fire insurance company sign bearing the date 1836. In the days when each insurance company employed its own fire detachment, signs were issued to its paid-up customers for quick identification of their houses.

At the next corner are three houses of special note, preserved and restored through the generosity of the late Mrs. Kathleen Drope. 135 Johnson, 240 Gate Street around the corner, and 243 which faces it, all date from the period after "the war". The last one, a neat little house beside One-Mile Creek, is known as the Slave Cottage.

This is the place to remind our readers (especially the Americans) that the legislature of Upper Canada, meeting in this town, abolished the importation of slaves in 1793. When the abolitionist fervour mounted in the States thirty or forty years later, many slaves escaped via the "underground railroad" to gain their freedom on this side of the Niagara River. Some found employment in our town and were housed in dwellings of this size. By the middle of the last century Niagara had a sizable Negro population, perhaps one-fifth of the total. Most of them apparently lived in the area beyond Mary Street.

A block and a half ahead stands the Clench house, built soon after the War of 1812 by Ralfe Clench, a prominent citizen who had been a lieutenant in Butler's Rangers. His house was the other one that escaped burning by the Americans. but it perished in a fire the following March, displacing two families. The present one faces south-east, parallel to Johnson, on a two-acre plot across which the One-Mile Creek meanders. This is a particularly elegant house in every way, and the property is one of the finest in town. Now retreat to the last corner and turn right onto Simcoe. If you are here when the trees are not in leaf, keep glancing to your right for a distant view of the front of the Clench house.

The elegant Clench house, viewed from the Simcoe Street side, with One-Mile Creek in the foreground. The side-hill site was skilfully used, making the basement entrance at ground level.

When you pass the corner of that property, however, on your right stands a neat-looking elevated bungalow, well back on its lot. It has not always been there. A few years ago it was an unoccupied derelict in danger of demolition, standing behind 590 Mississauga. Two people are responsible for rescuing it: one is the neighbour to the left, who purchased the old house, had it moved onto his property, and secured a severance; the other is the new owner, who arranged for the addition of a modern livable basement and a complete restoration. Its new cellarway at the right leads to a downstairs kitchen, and the meal may be conveyed to the diningroom directly over it by a dumb-waiter built into the wall.

The Butler house, a pleasant hip-roofed cottage, with broad centre hall and a symmetrical arrangement of rooms. Once a derelict on the former Butler lands, it was moved here and restored.

The two-storey house on the corner, made of scored stucco over brick, is also from the post-1812 period. The present owner, a permanent force army officer, had often been stationed at Camp Niagara, and knew the town well. He purchased the house in 1949, rented it out while he was posted elsewhere, and on retirement came back to live in the town he had always admired.

On the other side of Gage Street stands the Kirk Hall of St. Andrew's Church. Here too the army is with us, for the section of the building perpendicular to Simcoe started out in life as an army hut at the camp. At the end of World War II the Presbyterian congregation bought it and had it moved to this site. The wing that extends towards the church is an addition some five years old. As part of that project the army hut was also clad in brick, and the interior upgraded to make it a comfortable Kirk Hall whose origin is now skilfully camouflaged.

As to St. Andrew's itself, we are reluctant to launch into detail. Let this place of worship make its own impression on you. Enough to say that the Presbyterians secured this four-acre plot and built their first church in 1794. During the American occupation of the town it was unfortunately burned in the course of a raid in August 1813. The present church, rising in all its majesty in 1831, is very little changed from its original appearance. The foot-scrapers, the box pews, the precentor's desk and the elevated pulpit--all are there for the visitor to admire.

St. Andrew's Presbyterian Church, built in 1831, and the Kirk Hall. The section of the hall parallel to Gage Street was once an army hut at Niagara Camp.

Just past the church and on the left stands the Presbyterian manse, a well-preserved brick house. The Reverend Robert McGill, in whose time St. Andrew's was completed, had it built for himself. A later bequest from a member enabled the congregation to purchase the house as the residence for their minister.

The Creen house is located in the middle of the next block. It was built (c. 1817-1825) by John Breakenridge, a local lawyer, but for many years it was the home of the Reverend Thomas Creen, who succeeded Robert Addison at St. Mark's, and conducted a small private school here. A few years ago it was reconstructed--not actually restored, for it was beyond repair--with reasonable attention to its original plan. One unusual feature is the skylight, located over the stairway; by daytime it admits a useful light, and after dark the lights of the house shine heavenward through it.

Lately it has become fashionable hereabouts to build houses that **look** old, at least externally. One of these is next door to the Creen house, and another is around the corner of William Street to the right.

The Breakenridge-Hawley house displays what has been called "the most resplendent doorway in Niagara". The house and its coach-house occupy one of the original one-acre lots of the town.

But the house on the corner of William and Mississauga really is old, at least in terms of Upper Canada. This was John Breakenridge's second house, built about 1818 when he had come up in the world. The low building at the back, which you see first, was the coach-house; notice the three carriage-bays, with living quarters above. The house was purchased in 1954 by the present owner, who made its restoration a ten-year project. The doorway is particularly well-designed; even after dark the pleasant reddish glow that comes through the fanlight and side panels attracts the eye.

Turn right onto Mississauga and proceed one block. There, facing onto Centre Street, stands John Breakenridge's third house, this time in pink brick. It has four fireplaces on each floor, besides another and a bake-oven in the tall basement. At the moment its restoration is still proceeding.

Go one more block along Mississauga to the corner of Gage. (Be careful--there's no sidewalk here!) On the left side of Mississauga is a large clapboard house which at one time held still another of the town's private schools.

Now turn right onto Gage Street, along the fourth edge of the St. Andrew's property. To your right stand three large evergreens; examine the ground some twenty feet from the sidewalk and to the right of them, to find in the turf the traces of a simple stone foundation. On this site stood the Presbyterian meeting-house, a two-storey clapboard building apparently measuring about 25 feet by 35 feet. Erected soon after the first church, it housed their library and a schoolroom. Somehow the building escaped total destruction in the burning of the town, and till the 1831 church was built the Presbyterians conducted their services here. In the mid-1800s the upper floor was used as a schoolroom for Negro children, and much later the sexton made his home in the old meeting-house. When it deteriorated beyond repair it was finally taken down. Now there is nothing to mark its place except the few stones of its foundation.

In a few yards we pass the side of the Kirk Hall, and from here our route is straight ahead to King Street. In the first block past Simcoe it is worth noticing a brown house on the right, flush with the sidewalk, that was restored by a local craftsman quite recently. At the end of that block, look to the right, noting the tall house that is designed for solar heating. Across from it, behind a row of tall evergreens, is the Methodist cemetery which came into use about 1825. The meeting-house that stood nearby was moved down the street and is now a residence at the corner of Prideaux. We passed it near the end of Tour 2.

At the corner of Victoria an examination of the clapboard house on the left will reveal that it was originally two houses. The house to our right appears to have a finish of old brick; actually these are half-bricks cleverly pressed into a mortar base to make a better exterior wall with an antique appearance.

Two houses to the right of that one, at 315 Victoria, is a storey-and-a-half clapboard, built about 1850. Despite the solid-looking chimneys, it has no fireplaces; by that time the use of stoves for heating was becoming fashionable.

In the next block there is a contrast between the large white house on the left, still on its one-acre lot, and the modest homes opposite. Around 1800, when the town was young, it had a healthy mix of income groups, as reflected by their houses, and this is still the case. The next block also has a variety of houses, including one with a cone-shaped roof at the corner of King. On the right-hand corner stood Senator J.B. Plumb's sixteen-room mansion, complete with its own ballroom, but it was demolished thirty-five years ago to provide a school site.

Now turn left onto King Street, and in two blocks you will be back to the starting-point. If you admired the houses in this tour, please be aware that, unlike Williamsburg in Virginia, our community is not dependent on a generous benefactor for its continued existence as an historic town. The houses you saw have been preserved, maintained, and in some cases restored, by the efforts of private citizens.

To forget one's ancestors is to be a brook without a source, a tree without a root.

- Chinese proverb

YE BRIGHT LIGHTS
(8 blocks)

This is not our favourite tour, particularly in the summer, when the day-trippers are shuffling three or four abreast along the main street, clutching their ice-cream cones. Nevertheless anyone who can find Niagara-on-the-Lake invariably ends up on Queen Street. We feel it our duty therefore to start from the Prince of Wales corner, looking at the three commercial blocks and one residential block, observing the buildings and businesses that have something of special interest.

Queen Street itself is 99 feet wide, a chain and a half (so much for your metric measure!), because it was intended in the 1790s to be the main street. This dimension has turned out to be a boon in various ways. There is sufficient width to park, drive, and even pass, in both directions. Local drivers have learned to "come about" by making a U-turn anywhere on it, and do so freely. To the best of our knowledge, no one has been arrested for this. In the winter after a heavy snowfall the townspeople park along the middle line till the snowplough has done the curb lanes, then they move over to the edges. The street appears even wider because of the prohibition of overhead signs, a measure adopted by Town Council a few years ago.

But what is happening to Queen Street lately? Once it had a generous grassy boulevard along both sides. With the increase of tourists, however, another strip of sidewalk was put down beside the original one, then another beside the road, for those alighting from their cars. Each spring our Works Department faithfully renews the remaining strip of green, but by midsummer it has been trampled into submission.

The stores on Queen Street have increased in numbers but not always in quality. Several houses located there have had their ground floors remodelled to become shops. Two were moved away, in one case to provide more parking spaces, in another to be replaced by businesses. The commercial area has flowed around the corners, especially onto Victoria Street. The cost of buying or renting property on Queen Street has increased dramatically, causing some premises to be divided into two or more stores. See pages 52 and 54 for examples of these changes.

The situation is not all bad, of course. Two well-established firms are plying the same trade on the same premises as half-a-century ago. Some properties have been improved, some renovated, and a few even faithfully restored. These we shall point out. On the whole the service-type tradesmen – the butcher, the baker, the candlestick-maker – who are needed by townpeople for everyday shopping have become fewer, while the tourist-oriented shoppes have proliferated.

In Tour 1 we have already seen the Niagara Apothecary, a fine piece of restoration. Across the street stands a brick building which was the new fire hall in 1911. Our first recollection of the three-storey building next door was that of the dreadful penny arcade on the ground floor. Two local interior decorators attractively restored it to become "The Owl and the Pussycat". The liquor store next door was once a stationer's. The second storey was added so that it would not be dwarfed by the 1847 Court House. As the liquor store, it was revamped about ten years ago to assume an antique air, even to locating timber with wormholes for the arms of the turnstile. But business became so brisk that the turnstile was removed, leaving the old clock, the solid wood slab of the counter, and the roll-top desk in the office. This is the only liquor store in Ontario to have merited an official opening--but at its conclusion the dignitaries crossed the road to sip tea at the Buttery!

The children's shop of the left was built about 1830, and the "In-and-Out" store is somewhat younger. Both were restored some ten years ago.

From that side take a careful look at the broad wooden building to the right of the Court House, known as the Sherlock Block. Apparently there were originally (c. 1850) two separate buildings, alike in appearance. At some later date they were joined, with a new doorway between and a stairway to give access to the upper floor. The side roofs were extended inward to reach a high peak at the centre, with a new attic window. Finally, to disguise the wide sweep of the resulting roof-line, a false front was applied. The visual effect is now that of a frontier "boomtown" building.

A major reconstruction has taken place at the corner. The old Alma Block, a tall 1825 building of painted brick, was taken down and rebuilt to accommodate two stores on Queen, one on Regent, and the Niagara "Advance" around the back on Market Street, besides six comfortable apartments overhead. This project won an Ontario Renews Award in 1981.

On the other side of Regent is the Dee-LeDoux building, a pre-1850 structure that now houses a restaurant. The

Queen Street entrance is particularly solid, having cut-stone pilasters. The Regent Street front is perhaps more attractively designed, with its detailed doorway and flanking windows.

Tour 5
1. Former fire hall
2. Owl and the Pussycat
3. Liquor store
4. Court House
5. Sherlock Block
6. Dee-Ledoux Building
7. Greaves Jams
8. Royal George
9. Niagara Home Bakery
10. Grace United Church
11. McClelland's (to 1988)
12. Post Office
13. Former customs house
14. Rogers-Harrison house
15. McDougal-Harrison house
16. Crysler-Rigg house
17. Richardson-Kiely house

Across the road the second block begins with Greaves Jams, a long-established family concern. William Greaves set up in business here in 1927 from his farm just outside the old town, and using his wife's recipes began to make marmalade, jam, and preserves at the back of the store. Old Mr. Greaves died a couple of years ago, but at the last count eight of the family were still directly involved in the firm. The window-dressing is simple, but the delicious odours from the back room attract customers every time they come to town. While you're there, look behind the store at the small parking lot; the house that used to be there is now re-located at 390 Nassau Street.

A few doors down the street, the Royal George started out as a movie house called the "Kitchener" about the time of World War I. After the second war it was renamed the "Brock, and not too long ago the local mime troupe made

The "Royal George" at intermission time. Tastefully redecorated in 1978, it became the third stage for the Shaw. It has seating for 351 theatregoers.
(Photo courtesy Cosmo Condina)

This picture from the late 1870's shows the brick store at the corner of Queen and Victoria. The large T proclaims that William McClelland was a provisioner; notice the chickens in the windows? Today there are two stores in the brick building, and four in the wooden wing along Victoria Street.
(Photo Courtesy McClelland's)

it their home. Given a complete facelift in 1978, the Royal George is now the third stage for the Shaw Festival. Next door to it, a large house which occupied the corner was moved to 280 Dorchester, and we shall pass it near the end of Tour 8. This has made room for the Bank of Montreal and two shops, with some off-street parking behind them.

On the opposite side of Queen Street is the Niagara Home Bakery, another long-established business. In 1937 Paul Albrechtsen Sr. bought an ice-cream parlour here, and the bakery is still prospering under his sons John and Paul. The counter, furniture, and even the soda fountain have been retained, giving the interior of the store a pleasantly old-fashioned atmosphere.

Behind the Gulf Station stands a church that has served three denominations. It was built in 1853 for a group that left St. Andrew's Presbyterian, to a design by William Thomas, the architect who had planned our Court House a few years earlier. When the prodigals returned to St. Andrew's, the Methodists, whose 1823 frame church was showing signs of wear, rented the brick building for a couple of years. Eventually they purchased it for $1500, spent $750 on renovations, and dedicated their "new" church in 1878. (The wooden meeting-house, moved three blocks, is now a well-kept residence at 155 Gate Street.) A Sunday School room was built at the back of the church in 1888, to which has just been added a second storey containing a study and meeting-room. When church union came about in 1925, this Methodist congregation entered under the name of Grace United Church.

Soon after the War of 1812 McClelland's West End Grocery set up in business in a brick building at the corner of Queen and Victoria. In the 1870s they were able to expand into a second building next door to the original one. Lately, however, this old firm has fallen on hard times: a few years ago its business premises were confined to the second building. Then in 1988 the proprietor moved the business to an existing building at 170 Mary Street, still under the sign "McClelland's West End Grocery". At the time of writing, the area behind the store and the four offices upstairs are advertised for lease. Will the old firm of McClelland's become a thing of the past? If this happens it will be a matter for regret on the part of the townspeople and visitors alike.

The brick building next door was the new post office in 1951, but it outgrew these premises a few years ago. The federal government purchased Jayson's Hardware across the street, erected a new building there, and opened the present post office in June 1978. Two results quickly followed: the former post office was remodelled into a fudge shop, and Kennedy's Drug Store installed a new hardware section.

Further down the street, the black-and-white dry cleaner's premises was once a public building. Dating from about 1825, it later served as the Customs House during the time when William Kirby was the collector. With the flat top of its front wall surmounted by the royal coat of arms, it was undoubtedly an elegant building. It also has a certain literary connection, since Kirby formed the habit of returning to his office in the evening to work on his historical novel, "The Golden Dog", which was published in 1877.

Just before the corner we step back into early times once more. The historical plaque reminds us that the meeting to organize the Law Society of Upper Canada was held in Wilson's Hotel on this site in 1797. This is surprising, because that year the legislature began to hold its sessions in York, now Toronto. At any rate, the lawyers of the colony must have had an affection for Niagara, because they did not shift their headquarters across the lake to Osgoode Hall till 1832.

The building on the left was for many years the home of the Gollop family; now it holds two gift shops. The middle building has changed its occupants several times lately. The stone black-and-white dry cleaning establishment on the right was the local customs house in Victorian times, when William Kirby was the collector.

The brick MacDougal-Harrison house at 165 Queen Street shows two excellent features -- an elaborate doorcase, and the arcaded arches framing the windows on both floors.

In the next block we leave behind the business section of Queen Street to move into its residential district. The first two houses on the right were both built in the 1820s, and both have well-designed doorcases. The Rogers-Harrison house was originally clapboard, but was later covered with white stucco lined to look like stonework. The brick MacDougal-Harrison house next door has arcaded arches framing the windows in a manner seen in a few other old houses in town.

The distinction of the next house rests with its use rather than its age. This was the local "cottage hospital" for a number of years, and the house behind it was the nurses' residence. When our new hospital on the edge of the Commons was opened in 1951 the Queen Street building was made into apartments.

The white Crysler-Rigg house at 187 Queen dates from about 1822. It was originally called "Roslyn Cottage", an unusual title for so large a house, but the name may still be seen near the gate, in the sidewalk that was put down sometime before World War I. One of its early owners probably had the house modified to suit the Greek Revival style, and later the verandahs were added.

The Kiely House Heritage Inn, 209 Queen Street, gained approval from council to become a guest house in 1986. Notice the well-designed entrance and the Palladian window on the second floor.

On the other side of Simcoe Street is the Richardson-Kiely house, built in 1832, the only property that cuts into the golf club area. The original house was of symmetrical Georgian design, as may be detected from the front view. The addition to the right and the verandahs were added when Niagara became a popular holiday resort in late Victorian times.

The rest of Queen Street is covered in Tour 8. On the way back you may wish to follow the same route, looking at the shops again. If it was too crowded to be pleasant, you can always move one block towards the water to return by Prideaux, or one block away from it, returning by Johnson. In either case it is then four blocks back to King Street, with nothing but pleasant houses to engage your attention.

KING & REGENT
(14 blocks)

In this jaunt we will look at an elementary school with an unusual name; a popular hotel that started out as a canning factory; a well-known plant that produces fine yachts; and the normal quota of gracious older homes.

From the parking lot behind the Court House, turn right onto King Street. On your right stands a storey-and-a-half wooden building; between 1913 and 1931 it served as the ticket office for the electric railway to St. Catharines. The graceful turret is a recent addition, which greatly improved the appearance of the building. When the "trolley" ceased to run and the railway was later removed, King Street became unusually wide. In 1988 the extra land on the far side was used to make a generous grassy boulevard along the street.

King Street was originally the edge of the surveyed town. When the area to the east of it was developed later, it was decided that the new streets should not bear the names of the older ones, even though they were directly in line. Accordingly, at King Street Front became Ricardo; Prideaux became Byron; Queen became Picton; Johnson became Platoff; Gage became Castlereagh. Don't let it confuse you; this happens in Britain too!

Occupying the block between Gage and Centre stands Parliament Oak Public School, which in 1948 replaced the school we saw on Platoff. On the nearer wing of the school is a large carving depicting the opening of a session of the legislature of Upper Canada. A fine occasion indeed: there is Lieutenant-Governor John Graves Simcoe, around him are the assemblymen and councillors, and the mace is prominently displayed. But the background is filled with large trees. Why are they meeting out of doors?

The explanation appears on the farther wing of the building:

> "Upon this site according to historic records during a period of extremely hot weather in August 1793, one of the sessions of the first parliamenet of Upper Canada, which provided the basis for freedom and democracy in this Dominion, was held beneath a spreading oak tree under the chairmanship of Sir John Graves Simcoe. From this tree, which became known as 'Parliament Oak' and which for many years stood as a symbol of strength and stability, this school received its name."

But we also have consulted historical records, and they cast serious doubt on this description. The 1793 session lasted from May 31 to July 9, and by August Governor Simcoe was **not even in Niagara.** He and his family sailed for York (Toronto) on July 29, and they made it their headquarters for the rest of that year. Neither the Governor in his correspondence, nor Mrs. Simcoe in her diary, makes any mention of the oak tree or hot weather in August 1793. There is, in fact, **no** documentary evidence from that period that any session of the Upper Canada legislature was held under an oak tree.

Then where did they hold their meetings? The first, or 1792, session was probably held in the Freemasons' Hall, for Governor Simcoe ordered that a subaltern's guard be posted there on September 17, the day that session convened. As for the following four years, the dates of the sessions, and the acts passed, are well recorded, but not the meeting place. The lawmakers may have met in one of the buildings of Navy Hall, or at Butler's Barracks in the same area, or at Freemasons' Hall--perhaps in all three of these for various sessions. We can find no reason, and no hard evidence, for their meeting here, on what was then the edge of the town, especially under a tree.

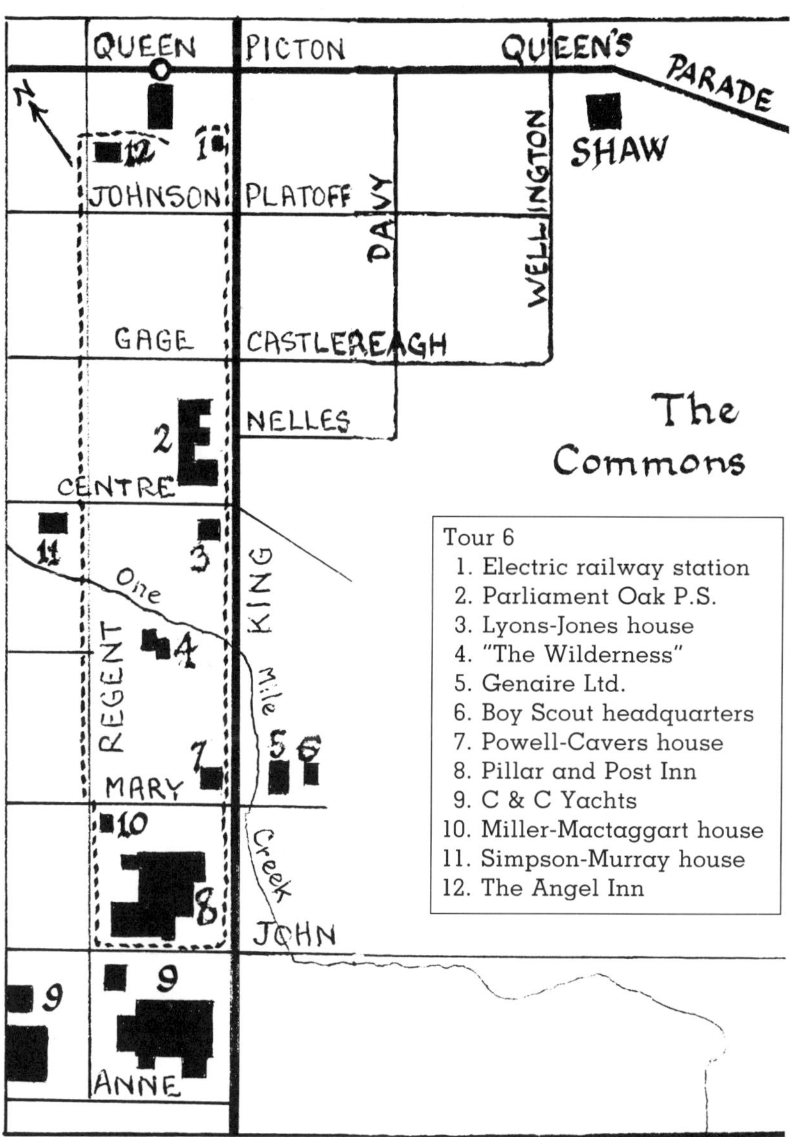

QUEEN
PICTON
QUEEN'S
PARADE
N
12
1
JOHNSON
PLATOFF
DAVY
WELLINGTON
SHAW
GAGE
CASTLEREAGH
The
Commons
NELLES
2 E
CENTRE
11
One
3
KING
Regent
Mile
4
7
5 6
MARY
10
Creek
8
JOHN
9
9
ANNE
Tour 6
1. Electric railway station
2. Parliament Oak P.S.
3. Lyons-Jones house
4. "The Wilderness"
5. Genaire Ltd.
6. Boy Scout headquarters
7. Powell-Cavers house
8. Pillar and Post Inn
9. C & C Yachts
10. Miller-Mactaggart house
11. Simpson-Murray house
12. The Angel Inn

The alert reader will have noticed two errors in the inscription that anyone can check from a standard history of Canada. "Sir" is a glaring mistake; John Graves Simcoe was never knighted. The claim that the legislature of Upper Canada "provided the basis for freedom and democracy in this Dominion" will infuriate any visitors from the Maritimes, for they will tell you that New Brunswick had had its own legislature since 1784, and Nova Scotia since 1758!

But where did the inscription come from? The answer is found on the low stone marker close to the sidewalk a few metres further on. Placed here by the Niagara Historical Society early this century, it reads:

> "ON THIS SPOT STOOD THE 'PARLIAMENT OAK' UNDER WHICH THE EARLY LEGISLATORS SAT ON ONE DAY IN SEPTEMBER 1792"

This inscription, direct but tantalizingly brief, is all the Society recorded. Our private opinion is that a few of the lawmakers set out for a walk at the end of a day's deliberations, and rested under said oak tree. In the re-telling the story improved steadily; finally someone convinced the Society that the incident should be immortalized by placing one of their stone markers nearby. (The oak tree died about that time!) The school board, looking for inspiration in the naming of their new school in 1948, seized on the simple inscription, moved the event from 1792 to 1793 while they embellished it beyond all recognition, and engraved **their** version for all to admire. At any rate, the school now has a unique name.

Across the road and fronting on Centre Street stands the Lyons-Jones house, built about 1835. This rough-cast house has a very fine doorway, and a well-designed though recent picket fence. The closed shutters on the front windows are an unusual feature, for there are no windows behind them. They cover the fireplace and the chimney stack, and were designed by the builder merely to give balance to the front of the house.

The next piece of property is one of the most unusual in town--a bungalow built right after the War of 1812, set in a four-acre woodlot with One-Mile Creek flowing through it. The house is suitably named "The Wilderness" and it is practically invisible from King Street in the summer. This property was given in the 1790s by the Indians to the widow of Daniel Claus as a mark of respect for her late husband, who had been Deputy Superintendent of the Indian Department at the end of the American Revolution. His son William succeeded him in this post, and local tradition tells us that the Indians drew up their canoes on the bank of the creek, much larger then, when they came to see him.

The Lyons-Jones house, 8 Centre Street, occupies a corner lot that slopes down the One-Mile Creek. The closed shutters cover no window: they are there to add balance to the front of the house.

Across the road stands a large grey building that houses part of a local industry, Genaire Limited. The company's main operation was organized at the St. Catharines Airport soon after the end of World War II to look after maintenance. overhaul, and repair of ground support equipment for the aviation industry. When the company expanded, a former Canadian Army transport building on this site was purchased. At present Genaire employs some 85 people in its two plants, most of them at the airport near Highway 55.

To see another example of a building being recycled, go left on the extension of Mary Street, past Genaire, and examine the white clapboard building. A church, you say? Yes--originally, but not now. This was the Niagara United

Mennonite Church, built in the mid-thirties on Highway 55 north of Virgil. In 1966 it was moved to this site to become the local Boy Scout building.

The corner of King and Mary is occupied by the Powell-Cavers house, a symmetrical two-storey home with a pleasantly-designed doorway. Built just after the War of 1812, this is actually a brick house covered with stucco, skilfully scored to appear like stone. On the other corner the red brick house, now an art gallery, displays carved keystones over the arches of its windows.

As you proceed along King Street, let your eye follow the course of the telegraph line as it bends to the left, finally disappearing through an opening in the trees on the far side of John Street. This was the route that the railway followed as it turned south towards the escarpment. The old right of way has become a footpath and trail-bike route.

Another busy day at the Pillar and Post! The two-storey section was originally a canning factory. The new entrance is in the foreground, and the motel rooms extend to the right.

At the corner of John, turn right and advance far enough to view the two-storey part of the Pillar and Post, a well-known inn. This was built in 1912 as a canning factory and operated successfully for perhaps forty years. Only fifteen years ago the building was a derelict, with broken windows, surrounded by ragged grass. A group of businessmen revitalized the old building: a diningroom and some accommodation were provided first, then additional wings to hold more guest rooms, a swimming pool, a handcraft shop, and meeting rooms. When the Queen and Prince Philip visited our town in June 1973, they made a stopover for dinner at the Pillar and Post before attending the Shaw Theatre. It has developed into a thriving year-round location for business conventions.

The block beyond John Street contains an industry of a very different sort. George Hinterhoeller, an Austrian-born boatbuilder, bought the property in 1963 to set up his own small factory. It prospered steadily, and seven years later became one the four companies that combined to form C&C Yachts. In 1983 this plant built 545 sailboats varying from 24 to 41 feet in length, valued at some $25,000,000. These are shipped to the retailers by road at any season, weather permitting. If you should meet a yacht on a tractor-trailer headed out of Niagara, it's sure to be a C&C product.

Part of C&C Yachts, with some of its products ready to be moved. The main buildings are behind the camera, and the new head office is to the right.

The company is still doing well. There are now six production lines, constructing boats between 27 and 44 feet long. Unlike tourism, C&C Yachts is a valuable year-round business, employing some three hundred workers from the town and the area. In June 1984 its head office moved from Port Credit into the new building across from the Pillar and Post. For 1987 C&C Yachts expects to produce between three and four hundred boats.

If you are a sailor, do walk an extra block up Regent Street, sniffing the ether and admiring the hulls parked in the yard. If you are especially keen to see how C&C Yachts produces a sailboat, you may phone 468-2101 to request a conducted tour of the plant.

At the corner of the Pillar and Post turn right onto Regent. The yellow storey-and-a-half house on your right at the corner of Mary is the Miller-Taylor house, which dates from 1817. Inside it has pine floors, corner cupboards, and seven fireplaces. The seventh occurs in the wing at the back; notice the chimney? The new garage and fence have been designed to match the original house.

This neat little house at 46 Mary Street was built for William D. Miller, who was an elder at St. Andrew's, owned a stationery store on Queen Street, and was an official at the Court House.

Cross Mary Street and continue down Regent. On the left at the end of the next block stands a large house, a funeral home since 1959, in which the Camp Niagara detachment of the Canadian Women's Auxiliary Corps was billeted during World War II. It faces across the road onto "The Wilderness" property. In this woodlot, a few yards short of One-Mile Creek, stands one of the biggest oak trees in this area, honoured with a brass plaque stating its dimensions.

Move ahead from the corner of William Street, and over the creek, past the old rail fence on your left. As you approach the corner of Centre Street, look to your left to admire the side of the fine property that slopes down towards the creek. It's worth while to turn left onto Centre and enjoy the front view of the house. This was the residence of John Simpson, a businessman who rose in local politics to become mayor of Niagara, 1852-6. Entering the provincial scene, he represented Niagara till 1864, when he was appointed deputy auditor general for Canada West (Ontario).

Continuing along Regent, we pass behind Parliament Oak School. The houses in this block and the next may not be architecturally distinguished, but they are certainly all different from each other. When you reach Johnson you will realize that this is the corner you passed on the way to St. Andrew's Church.

Press on past the bowling green towards Queen Street. Just before you reach it, look up at the third floor of the Alma Block. The porch that is part of that upper apartment was not present in the original building, but was cleverly added in the reconstruction. Turn right onto Market Street at the Angel Inn. This is one of our smaller hotels, built about 1825, comfortable and homey in atmosphere. From here the walk to the parking lot provides you with another view of the back part of the Court House.

This tour has illustrated some of the changes that have taken place in Niagara. The railroad, the electric railway, and the canning factory ceased operating some years ago. On the other hand, newer businesses like Genaire, C&C Yachts, and the Pillar and Post have sprung up to take their place, two of them in buildings that once had a very different use.

MOSTLY MILITARY
(15 blocks)

The place to start this tour is the small parking lot just beside John Street. Drive out King Street as far as the Pillar and Post, then turn left onto John. The first street on your right is Charlotte; at that point turn left into the parking lot, and leave your car there.

Before we look at the evidence of the military story of our town, there is a rural and residential aspect right next to it that should be noticed. On the other side of John Street stands a pleasant board-and-batten storey-and-a-half house of symmetrical design. Built about 1860, it was a farmhouse a generation ago, and still seems at home in its rural setting among the trees. Some yards to the right stands its disused and weatherbeaten barn.

This house and the two to the left of Charlotte Street all stood on the spacious estate of the Dickson family. William Dickson was a Scot who came out just after the American Revolution and built the first brick house in Niagara. When the Americans burned the town in 1813 he lost everything, including a large personal library, but he was nevetheless able to build two fine houses on John Street after peace returned. These appeared on town maps as "Rowanwood" and "Woodlawn" for many years. To look at the Dickson holdings, let's walk out John Street, keeping to the sidewalk in front of the wall.

The first driveway past Charlotte Street led to Rowanwood. It was demolished some years ago, to be replaced by the large white clapboard house on the same site. Woodlawn still exists, however, and you can get a good view of it from the third entrance. It was built in 1825 as a two-storey brick house with end chimneys; the mansard roof was a mid-Victoria alteration, and the belvedere another at the turn of the century. In 1905 the property was bought by George Rand, an American, and the house was re-named "Randwood". The front of the property is beautifully landscaped, with the upper waters of One-Mile Creek flowing through it. At the back there is a huge shaded lawn for garden-parties, a tennis-court, and a secluded guest house.

Randwood, at 120 John Street, is now leased to the Niagara Institute. One-Mile Creek, scarcely visible from here, flows across the lawn, widening into a circular pond at the walkway.

At the present time, however, neither of these properties is a residence. In 1976 the Niagara Institute secured the lease of the two buildings and the thirteen acres of grounds as a centre for executive seminars attended by government, business, and labour personnel. The interior of both houses has been modified somewhat for this purpose, and the whole environment now provides an ideal setting for study and discussion.

Here is Brunswick Place, home of Captain Robert Melville, to whom we owe the origins of the present marina at Niagara. Like other local homes, it was enlarged during the late Victorian period.

Still further out John Street, the next house is "Brunswick Place", built in the 1830s for Captain Robert Melville. He was the prime mover in the establishment of the Harbour and Dock Company, which was mentioned already in Tour 2. This house was enlarged during the Victorian period, and it too is a most attractive residence.

At this point, cross the road and turn back until you come to a driveway that crosses the ditch. Turn right, and some twenty metres onto the Commons turn left onto a gravel track with trees on both sides. You are now treading a camp road that has felt the measured rhythm of thousands of military feet. Four minutes' steady marching will bring you opposite the parking lot; do a smart left wheel to reach it once more.

This large area north of John Street and east of King was set aside by the British government as a military reserve at the time of settlement by the Loyalists. It is now, of course, federally-owned. Remember the first Butler's Barracks, whose site is now marked by a plaque that we read on Tour 2? Fort George was so badly damaged by the American bombardment in the spring of 1813 that Britain not only began Fort Mississauga but also determined to establish a new barracks beyond the range of the cannon of Fort Niagara. Accordingly, in the period after the War of 1812 a new cluster of buildings gradually arose on the military reserve. It seemed appropriate to use the name of Butler's Barracks again, for the exploits of the Rangers were still recalled with pride.

Now follow the arrow "Historic Walking Tour Begins" from the parking lot and read your way around, using the printed displays provided by Parks Canada. The position of each of the buildings of Butler's Barracks is shown by a ridge of turf to outline it, and the various uses to which that building was put are listed on the sign beside the path. You will presently come to a large metal model which depicts the whole complex as it was in the 1850s.

The author pauses to admire the restoration done by Parks Canada at Butler's Barracks. At the right are the men's barracks, then the ordnance gunshed and the commissariat store.

This was its most flourishing period, as one might guess by the number and variety of buildings. The palisade shown was not intended as a defensive work, but rather as a way of defining and enclosing the barracks area. You will notice, however, that a few of the buildings were located outside it. Since the troops here were responsible for Fort Mississauga, detachments of infantry and artillery were regularly despatched there as a garrison. Fort George was of interest only as an historical ruin during this period.

Of the buildings shown on the model, only four have survived, which appear as numbers:

6 - the men's barracks (1817), the two-storey building on

your right, with end chimneys and an outside
stairway to the second floor;

12 - the ordnance gunshed (1821), a low building with three
cannon parked nearby;

11 - the commissariat store and office (1831), a
two-and-a-half storey building to your front left.

Ordnance Gunshed (1821)

The fourth one, the commissariat officer's quarters, is not quite in plain view from here, but you may reach it by proceeding about a hundred metres past the gunshed. When you find it, walk around to the front, for the building faces north-east.

This is a one-storey structure, of which the brick kitchen at the left rear was originally separate. When it was built in 1817 this was considered a safety measure, because a fire that got out of control in the kitchen might otherwise destroy the whole building. Besides being used by the military, this old bungalow later saw a variety of other uses: at the turn of the century it was the clubhouse for the golf club when their 18-hole course was on the Commons; it was the clubhouse for the Lions for a few years; and under the ownership of the Town, it has been used as a meetingplace for various local organizations. The commissariat officer's quarters has quite recently been acquired by Parks Canada, and its restoration is now taking place.

The restoration of the commissariat officer's quarters began in earnest in the summer of 1984. A couple of years later it looked like this, the exterior complete and the building neatly fenced in.

Walk back to the gravel path and continue around it. Within a few yards a tree-lined wagon track leads across the Commons in the direction of Fort George. Go along it some four hundred metres and look for a low grey marker to the right, just before a grove of trees. Placed here by the Niagara Historical Society, this indicates the site of the Indian Council House in the period around 1800. Later the building was converted into a military hospital serving Butler's Barracks, and finally perished in a fire about 1880. A few metres further ahead, where the little stream cuts across the wagon track, the Engineers built a cement bridge, and left their own inscription on it, "R.C.E. - 1913". From here you will need to retrace your steps along the wagon track until you reach the gravel path once more.

Before that time, however, political decisions elsewhere had brought about changes that affected Niagara. Soon after the Dominion of Canada was formed in 1867, a new British government decided that our country ought to be responsible for its own defence, and soon the British regulars were recalled from Canada. As a result the Canadian government designated four centres for training the militia, and Camp Niagara was one of these.

The first units arrived here by steamer from Toronto in the summer of 1872, to occupy neat rows of bell tents on the edge of the Commons for their sixteen days of drill and manoeuvres. For Niagara this was something of a godsend. This steady flow of summer visitors in the colourful uniforms of their various units generated considerable local business in the matter of supplies and services, as well as the sale of souvenirs to take home. For the young militiamen it was a stimulating change: a free trip by steamer or rail, an active programme in a pleasant environment, and a town only a step away where they might spend the evening when the day's training was over.

An artillery concentration at Camp Niagara in late Victorian times. The guns are lined up to the left of the wagon in the foreground, and the ammunition limbers are to their right.

This routine continued with few variations for nearly a century. Some of the buildings of Butler's Barracks were replaced by newer ones, and khaki became the dominant colour after the Boer War. About that time there was a strong move to abandon Camp Niagara because of its limited size, but it was saved, much to the joy of the townspeople, when the federal government acquired a large area along the Lake Ontario shore in 1908, and set up the rifle range on it. This was an opportune move, because the camp facilities were soon pressed to the limit during World War I. Near the end of that war, as already mentioned in Tour I, Camp Niagara also accommodated the Polish force for its basic training.

At some time or other every branch of the army was represented at this camp. Nor was it merely a militia base: during the 1930s the Royal Canadian Dragoons and the Royal Canadian Regiment, both permanent force units,

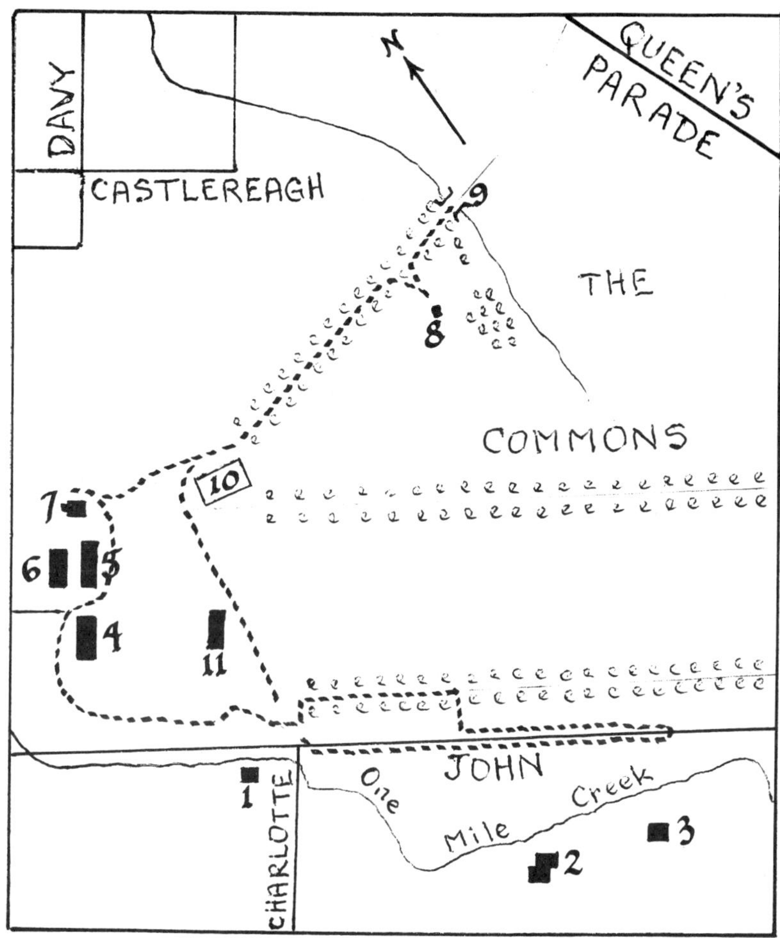

Tour 7
1. Dickson-Potter house
2. Randwood
3. Brunswick Place
4. Men's Barracks
5. Ordnance Gunshed
6. Commissariat Store
7. Commissariat Officer's Quarters
8. Indian Council House and Military Hospital (site)
9. Engineers' bridge
10. Parade square
11. World War II building

were regularly posted here during the summer. The horses of the Dragoons added a lively touch to field manoeuvres, and as a diversion they even organized polo games. When World War II was approaching, horses were replaced by motorized vehicles, and on the declaration of war Camp Niagara was once more the scene of vigorous activity. The town itself was hard-pressed to supply accommodation for visitors and for those service personnel who had living-out privileges.

Where the wagon track approaches the gravel path, look for the World War II parade square on your left, and as you pass it, turn left onto the path again. There is a plan of Camp Niagara in 1943 on the third-last display board, showing a great number of buildings. When the war finished, however, the camp was finally judged to be too small; some buildings were sold and towed away, others demolished. A few of them, as we have already mentioned in earlier tours, are still around town in various disguises. One only, which somehow escaped this fate, has lately been moved to a site near this part of the path, and bears the sign "Company B Headquarters."

After a quiet spell Camp Niagara was reactivated in 1953 for militia training. Its appearance then is recorded in the second-last display, an aerial view looking towards John Street. This time the camp appears to be composed overwhelmingly of bell tents and marquees. At the lower right corner, however, three of the Butler's Barracks buildings--the commissariat stores, the gunshed, and the men's barracks--may still be seen.

One other unique use of the military reserve must be mentioned. In 1955 the Eighth World Scout Jamboree was held at Niagara, and once more it sprouted a forest of bell tents for a few days while lads from all corners of the earth gathered here. Summer militia training continued on a reduced scale till 1967, but since then the detachments of militia have carried out their practices on the area along the lakeshore.

Today there is little evidence of the former use of the area as a military camp. Tarmac roads have been replaced by turf, and cement footings have been broken up and removed. The last display board, however, does bear pictures of the cap badges of many of the units which trained at Camp Niagara.

That area is now generally called the "Commons". It provides a pleasant green belt for the town, a place to exercise a dog, fly a kite, or pick mushrooms at dawn. The townspeople have resisted any suggestion to abandon it to the developer, though there are certainly seven pieces which have been put to other necessary uses during the last half-century: the new housing area after World War II alongside King Street; the Shaw Festival Theatre and the right-of-way for Queen's Parade, both in 1973; Simcoe Hall, the senior citizens' apartments; the Fort George parking lot beside Queen's Parade; and lately Upper Canada Lodge, in 1988. There is also one other, the small parking lot just ahead where you left your car. See you on Tour 8!

". . . the ignorance of Toronto people about our town is stupendous; we need not talk of the British or U.S. ignorance of Canada".

Janet Carnochan, President of the
Niagara Historical Society, writing
to David Boyle, Provincial Archaeo-
logist, 28 April 1903

THE CHAUTAUQUA AND LAKESHORE
(13 km - 8 miles)

Because of its length, this tour deserves to be done by automobile. It can be covered on a bicycle, however, because the land hereabouts is mostly flat, and the distance is not excessive. For those who wish to do it in two outings, a place is suggested where the tour might be divided. No bicycle? You may rent one at the Pillar and Post, even if you're not staying there.

This tour will take you around the edge of town along the Lake Ontario shore, through a Victorian suburb, past the rifle range, a couple of new parks, and some fruit farms, with a look at Butler's Burying Ground on the way back. The starting-point is the corner of Queen and Simcoe Streets, where you turned around on Tour 5. From there, drive or pedal out Queen Street, heading north-west.

Along this stretch are some of the finest properties in town, intermingled with some quite modest homes. All of them enjoy a pleasant view of the golf course, with the lake in the distance. On the right the original fourth hole of the course used to stretch 585 yards parallel to Queen Street. Within the last couple of years, however, when the club modified the course at the request of Parks Canada (see page **28**) it was divided into two holes of 475 and 140 yards.

At the end of Queen Street, park for a few moments to read the inscription on the cairn. Here in brief is the story of the capture of Niagara in 1813, though it is something of a misnomer to call it "The Battle of Fort George". The crucial part of the battle was fought on the shore, a mile or more to the west, where the Americans made their landing, opposed by a force of British regulars, Canadian militia, and Indians. Once ashore, the invaders were able to form up and advance towards the town. The defenders, badly outnumbered, made a stand here and there, spiked the

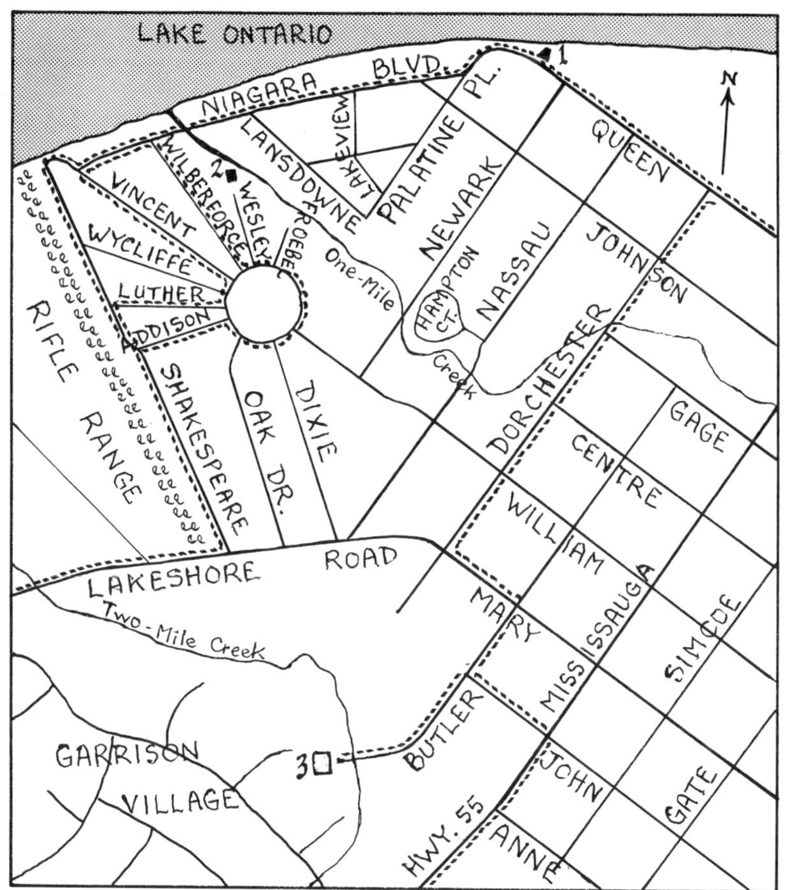

Tour 8
1. Cairn: Battle of Fort George   3. Butler's Burying Ground
2. Lewis Peake's house

guns of Fort George, and retreated in good order towards Queenston.

But there is evidence close at hand that the battle passed this way. Notice the low stone marker to the right of the cairn, placed there early this century by the historical society.

> "Here were found in August 1899 the remains of three soldiers who fell on May 27th, 1813, in defence of our country."

This was never a regular graveyard; it is therefore likely that these soldiers were buried close to where they died.

From here go carefuly around the blind curve onto Niagara Boulevard. This is a pleasant area: all the houses on the right have a fine view of Lake Ontario, but sometimes they are buffeted by a gale from the north. Four or five blocks ahead the road dips to pass over what appears to be a weedy lagoon, but which is actually the mouth of One-Mile Creek. Once across, pull in to the right and park, to hear the story of the Niagara Chautauqua.

When the Americans fought their way ashore in this area, the farm of James Crooks was so badly devastated that he abandoned it, and his land lay unused until the 1880s. Then Lewis Peake, a Toronto man, and Robert Warren, our local postmaster, set out to develop a summer chautauqua similar to that of Jamestown, New York, They acquired the 92 acres of "Crookston" and laid out streets like the spokes of a wheel, radiating from a central circle which was reserved for an amphitheatre reputedly capable of seating four thousand people. The stated aim of the Niagara Chautauqua was:

> "The establishment and maintenance of a summer resort
> under Religious, Temperance and Educational auspices,
> for Literary, Social, and Scientific purposes."

Those who attended its early meetings lived in tents and summer cottages, but within a few years some of the "regulars" had built handsome houses. Two are within sight, back at the corner of Wilberforce and the Boulevard. When Lewis Peake brought his furniture across the lake on a barge, it was able to enter One-Mile Pond (which was then named Lake Lansdowne, in honour of our governor-general) and deliver it to the door of his house beside the inlet. Though the Chautauqua season ran only from mid-June to mid-September, two hotels were built to accommodate the visitors.

The Niagara Chautauqua offered a wide range of courses, lectures, and concerts. In addition, a regular and well-attended Sabbath service was held in the amphitheatre. Various recreational facilities were also provided: there was a bowling green, croquet lawn, and a baseball diamond; the level area to the right of the road just ahead once held a tennis-court; beyond it a wharf extended into the lake, for the convenience of the sailors; and the sandy beach was there for all to enjoy.

Travelling to and from the Chautauqua presented no problem. At that time the steamers "Cibola" and "Chicora" were each making two trips across the lake every day. The Michigan Central, alert for new business, offered fare-and-a-third return from any station in Canada for passengers attending the Niagara Chautauqua. A spur line was laid across town to a station near the corner of William and Nassau Streets; from there the local train ran to the Niagara dock to make connections with both the Toronto steamers and the Buffalo trains.

In 1891, when the town waterworks building was completed, running water and electric lights were extended to the Chautauqua area. Its grounds were not open to all comers, however: any outsiders who wished to attend paid a ten-cent admission fee, except on Sunday. There were two gates, one at the station, the other near the corner of Johnson and the Niagara Boulevard.

Unfortunately, the hopes of the Chautauqua organizers were dashed soon after on the rocks of finance, due apparently to a misunderstanding about their local tax assessment. Another company took over, and very shortly the spur line was removed and the electric light poles were taken down. The ambitious summer programme was abandoned, though the area continued to be popular as a summer resort. The final blow came on 25 August 1909, when the Chautauqua Hotel burned to the ground.

Chautauqua Hotel, about 1890, located to the east of One-Mile Creek. Its rates were $2.00 to $2.50 a day, or $10 to $14 a week.

Since then the unoccupied property has been sold for building lots, including the circle itself, though there remains a pedestrian right-of-way across it. A very few of the original families still live there, but at least the streets run where they were laid out, and their interesting names remind us of the inspirational aims of the Niagara Chautauqua.

Today this area contains a very mixed bag of dwellings. There are a few mid-Victorian houses, but also some that started out as summer cottages and still look the part. Others have been added to, insulated, and upgraded into year-round homes. In some cases the original cottages have been demolished and replaced by well-designed modern houses. Unlike the older part of Niagara, the neighbours here must live at close quarters, since the lots are smaller and necessarily of odd shapes.

Now go ahead to the three-way stop, and turn right, around the curve onto Shakespeare. If you hear bursts of small-arms fire close at hand don't be alarmed, for behind the screen of trees on your right is the Department of National Defence rifle range. About three hundred metres ahead turn left onto Addison, past "Harmony Hall" of the local Lions Club, to the stop sign. Turn right, but then bear left in order to go around the circle. The local Works Department has labelled this street "Chautauqua Amphitheatre", surely a name of record length, but also one which preserves its origin. The telephone directory is content to call it simply "Circle", and that is how the townspeople refer to it.

Most of the way around it, a short dead-end street named Wesley leads to Lewis Peake's house. Just past it, turn right onto Wilberforce, noting the style of numbers 8 and 18. When you reach Niagara Boulevard again, turn left, and at the three-way stop this time turn left onto Vincent. At the circle once more, turn right and take the second turn to your right, which is Luther. Number 8, though not large, is one of the early Chautauqua houses. The present owners recently unearthed a slab in their front yard with the inscription "The Pagoda" on it. Numbers 9 and 10 are also of that period. At the end of Luther turn left onto Shakespeare and continue to the stop sign at the Lakeshore Road.

If at this point you are running a little low in time (or energy) you may wish to turn back here, doing the rest of this tour later. Simply turn left onto Lakeshore Road, which will bring you back onto Mary Street, and thus into town. For the other half of this tour, make your way to this corner by the shortest route, and continue out the Lakeshore.

Now turn right onto Lakeshore Road for still another look at the military side of our town. Within a few yards the rifle range appears on your right. This can accommodate twenty marksmen on its firing-points for practices of up to six hundred yards, though it uses only a portion of the 380 acres that the Department of National Defence acquired early this century. The rest of this extends westward, between the Lakeshore Road and the lake.

Since 1967, as was mentioned in the last tour, the militia units have trained on this area rather than the Commons. They make their headquarters in the large barn, using its lower level as the mess hall, and pitch their tents in the grassy area beyond it. The largest concentration here occurred in August 1976, when seven units sent 400 of their personnel (including 75 women) for a week's training.

On the other side of Lakeshore Road the new development of Garrison Villge appears. This is a typical suburban layout, with curving roads and crescents where there used to be grapevines. On the Lake Ontario side a sizable pond comes into view, not yet fully screened by the young trees that border the road. The sign announces that this is our Pollution Control Lagoon, actually a settling basin with a built-in sewage treatment facility. It was formed some twenty years ago by damming back the lower course of Two-Mile Creek, which used to meander through a marshy area there that provided an informal wildlife refuge.

Outdoor instruction for a squad of the Royal Hamilton Light Infantry. To the left is the barn; on the skyline by the tents are the target numbers of the rifle range.

This soon gives way to a semi-open area, well posted with D.N.D. signs, where the militia practise fieldcraft and platoon tactics. Across from this begins a succession of small farmhouses, many of them with orchards behind them. The old road diverges to the left, leaving a picnic area between it and the Lakeshore Road.

Watch for the sign "Niagara Shores Conservation Area" on the right, and turn onto the gravel road there. Some three or four hundred metres will bring you to a small parking lot, a good place to stop and look around. The level area to your left used to house the buildings of the mental health camp. of which the only remaining evidence is a lonely-looking pump. From the top of the bluff you can enjoy a panoramic view of Lake Ontario. If there are cargo vessels moving westward, they are bound for the entrance to the Welland Canal, some six kilometres away, or perhaps the docks at Hamilton, at the end of the lake.

Speaking of mental health, why not take the footpath that leads down to the beach, and enjoy a barefoot walk in the sand? To your left you can stroll to the mouth of Four-Mile Creek, and the beach to your right is even longer. This Niagara Shores area was leased by the Department of National Defence to the Niagara Peninsula Conservation Authority and opened in 1983 as a day use area. The few picnic tables near the pump are a mere beginning in the plans for its development. Most of our visitors haven't found it, but you can enjoy its serenity now.

As you leave Niagara Shores, turn right, and just ahead, where the road dips to cross a small creek, turn sharp left onto the old road. At the stop sign turn right onto Niven Road. For a short distance there is a rough treed area by the creek bed on your right, then a level picnic area that is only lately being discovered by visitors. This gives way to an area of fruit farms, with the road winding in general conformity to the course of the creek. Where Upper Canada Drive joins it from the left, you are once more within view of Garrison Village. The last piece of Niven Road is straight, with neat rows of fruit trees or grapevines on either side.

Where Niven Road reaches Highway 55, known locally as the Niagara Stone Road, turn left towards the town. Notice the contrast between the well-tended grapevines on the right and the neglected ones on the left, which will disappear when Garrison Village expands this far. Soon the road dips into the narrow ravine of Two-Mile Creek, with the miniature golf course on the right. The next building on the other side originally housed a small winery, then it produced circuit plates for thirty years, but lately it was closed down by the parent company. However, right next door is a very recent venture, the Tree Line Farm equestrian centre, which is doing well.

As you enter the town, turn left onto John Street, one block before the traffic lights. The small saltbox house, 507 Butler Street, that faces you at the end of the block was built about 1835. This must have been before this part of the town was properly surveyed, for its right edge infringes on the unopened road allowance. Now turn left at the corner and proceed to the end to look at Butler's Burying Ground.

This is part of the land grant that Colonel John Butler received when his Rangers were disbanded in 1784. His farmhouse, long vanished , stood on the banks of Two-Mile Creek about a hundred metres this side of Highway 55. The first plaque gives a brief biography of Butler, and the inscription on the stone marker tells about a skirmish at Butler's Farm on 8 July 1813, when the Americans were still in possession of the town. Notice that the engagement, in which the Americans sustained some casualties, was largely carried out by our Indian allies.

This was a family burying ground, an institution not at all uncommon in the early days of Upper Canada. Here lie buried the Butlers, some in-laws, and some close friends. When Butler himself died in 1796, he was interred here by the Reverend Robert Addison; unfortunately, the location of his grave was forgotten, and no stone was ever erected to mark it.

Over the years his land passed into other hands, and the old cemetery was neglected. In 1904 the United Empire Loyalist Society branches from Toronto, St. Catharines, and Hamilton made a special outing to Niagara, and naturally asked to visit Butler's Burying Ground. Even with the aid of guides from the local historical society, they had to push their way through undergrowth to find it.

Butler's Burying Ground is an early family cemetery, located on Colonel John Butler's land grant. There is unfortunately no gravestone for him, since the location of his grave somehow went unrecorded.

About 1920 the Niagara Parks Commission undertook to protect this cemetery by erecting a stout iron fence around it. As a centennial project in 1967 the N.P.C. went further, assembling the old gravestones in the centre of the site, and placing a new marker for each of them. The burying ground is well-kept, and the U.E.L. descendants who come today will find it without difficulty.

On the way back into town let's look at another neighbourhood. Go back along Butler, and at the stop sign on Mary, turn left for one block, then right onto Dorchester. In the first couple of blocks the houses are like those in any other subdivision. As you cross One-Mile Creek, however, the weathered little barn on your right and the neat clapboard house beside it are of an earlier vintage.

The large buff-coloured house beside it has been moved, not once, but twice! Originally it stood on the south-east corner of Simcoe and Queen, then in 1914 it was moved onto the back end of the site now occupied by the Bank of Montreal and its two neighbours. In 1973 many of us watched it being towed along Queen Street on a large carrier, to be set on a new foundation where it now stands. (Moving a wooden house of this size is not as difficult as one would imagine: the chimneys, which are the heaviest part, must be taken down first, and reconstructed after the move.) The house was then entirely done over, and the garage designed to blend with it.

One block further on, turn right at the stop sign. There's Fort Mississauga across the golf course, and away along Queen Street is the Clock Tower, both familiar landmarks to you by now.

All that remains is for me to say, "Hope you enjoyed going around our town with me. Happy travelling!"